A continuation of the serendipitous saga commenced in *RAVING VIOLET*, Valerie Gilbert's first non-fiction collection of short stories, *MEMORIES, DREAMS & DEFLECTIONS: My Odyssey Through Emotional Indigestion*, picks up the sojourn of this sassy, single mystic, mired in her mind and cloistered above the streets of New York City.

This volume explores Valerie's intrepid and irreverent search for healing inside and out (both medical and mystical), the quest for peace (and quiet) and, as always, true love.

PRAISE for Valerie Gilbert

Mirthamystic Miss! Healing Bliss! Valerie Gilbert is hilarious. I have done stand-up for years and her writing qualifies as brilliant stand-up comedy philosophy, with "prevailer" life skills. As an actress and observer of life, she blends pathos and compassionate "snark" to weave a great story. Read her, grow wiser, and be happy that one person has a grasp on modern culture. Annie Lamott and Valerie Gilbert can cover the coasts for me any time. She is an original OPTIMYSTIC! – *Michael Pritchard, PBS host and commentator, featured in documentary* Happy.

I've been surprised at just how strongly I've been drawn to her work, but am now seeing more clearly why. She's so REAL, with such an unabashed authenticity, and I find that to be magnetic and refreshing. Too many masks/facades still in our society, so genuineness shines like a beacon! – *Frances James, Australia*

VALERIE IS GREAT! After reading only a few sentences, I had a smile on my face that turned to a chuckle and burst into a full blown laugh. This continued through to the very last word. I haven't had so much fun for a long time, and enjoyed every minute of it. – *Larry Burton, Indy 500 mechanic, pilot, veteran*

ACKNOWLEDGEMENTS

With love and appreciation to Ms. Bridgett Walther, who continues to be mentor, pal, staunchest supporter, cheerleader, and inspiration.

Great gratitude to the good people of Black Opal Books, Lauri, Jack, LP, Susan, Faith, Arwen, and Daniel. Thank you for your continued support and partnership.

Also by Valerie Gilbert

RAVING VIOLET

Released by Black Opal Books on January 18, 2013

MEMORIES, DREAMS & DEFLECTIONS:

MY ODYSSEY THROUGH EMOTIONAL INDIGESTION

BY VALERIE GILBERT

A BLACK OPAL BOOKS PUBLICATION

GENRE: NON-FICTION/MEMOIRS/HUMOR

This book is a work of non-fiction. All information and opinions expressed herein are the views of the author. This publication is intended to provide accurate and authoritative information concerning the subject matter covered and is for informational purposes only. Neither the author nor the publisher is attempting to provide legal advice of any kind.

MEMORIES, DREAMS, AND DEFLECTIONS: My Odyssey Through Emotional Indigestion
Copyright © 2013 by Valerie Gilbert
All Rights Reserved
Cover Design by Valerie Gilbert
Cover and author photos by Valerie Gilbert
Copyright © 2014 All Rights Reserved
Print ISBN: 978-1-626941-02-1

First Publication: JANUARY 2014

All rights reserved under the International and Pan-American Copyright Conventions. No part of this book may be reproduced or transmitted in any form or by any means, electronic or mechanical, including photocopying, recording, or by any information storage and retrieval system, without permission in writing from the publisher.

WARNING: The unauthorized reproduction or distribution of this copyrighted work is illegal. Criminal copyright infringement, including infringement without monetary gain, is investigated by the FBI and is punishable by up to 5 years in federal prison and a fine of $250,000.

ABOUT THE PRINT VERSION: If you purchased a print version of this book without a cover, you should be aware that the book is stolen property. It was reported as "unsold and destroyed" to the publisher, and neither the author nor the publisher has received any payment for this "stripped book."

IF YOU FIND A PRINT VERSION OF THIS BOOK BEING SOLD OR SHARED ILLEGALLY, PLEASE REPORT IT TO: lpn@blackopalbooks.com.

Published by Black Opal Books: **http://www.blackopalbooks.com**

DEDICATION

To my Muse, Mimi Luisa.

TABLE OF CONTENTS

Introduction..1

CHAPTER 1:
Make Me Happy..7

CHAPTER 2:
Making Peace..17

CHAPTER 3:
Lean On Me...28

CHAPTER 4:
How to Give a Bad Psychic Reading..............................34

CHAPTER 5:
The Big Black Box..54

CHAPTER 6:
M'ama Non M'ama..70

CHAPTER 7:
Still Waters..80

CHAPTER 8:
Iced Coffee..91

CHAPTER 9:
Twisted..101

CHAPTER 10:
The Flood..113

CHAPTER 11:
Three Sisters..123

CHAPTER 12:
Forgive Me Not..135

CHAPTER 13:
Candy-Assed Dating..151

CHAPTER 14:
Sacred Geometry..158

CHAPTER 15:
Mama Rules...165

CHAPTER 16:
The Hand Off...171

CHAPTER 17:
Thanks, But No Thanks...181

CHAPTER 18:
A Day in the Country..190

CHAPTER 19:
Falling Together..202

CHAPTER 20:
Chasing Rainbows in a Hurricane................................225

CHAPTER 21:
Hysteria, Redux...231

INTRODUCTION TO MOI

Who am I? Rather, who the *hell* am I? Why do I curse, rant, and rave when I claim to be New Age? How can someone spouting peace and love still be so judgmental? I'll tell you why, and it's central to my spiritual tenets and who I am. Because I don't believe that when you cleave to love and light that you toss out discernment. In fact, we rely on it to get by in this world. I don't think that to become more loving you must eviscerate your personality or your preferences. In fact, what you choose and how you see the world determines who you are.

As we uplift our energies and merge with the higher dimensional aspects of our selves (I guess we meet in the middle, huh? Maybe that's the balance that the Star of David represents?) we do not toss out the human component. In fact, the human is as vital to the soul as the soul is to the human. Also, when a channeled spirit (whom I trusted implicitly) referred to my ex-husband as a jerk (which shocked the heck out of me), I figured, if Spirit can call a spade a spade then so can I, dammit! I'm guessing he said this to shock me out of my sad stupor, vulnerability, and semi-recumbent doormat status. It helped. Being nice doesn't mean you have to be a sucker.

And some people really are jerks. I don't care how clean their souls are. If they're not acting from a place of love and light, I am not turning the other cheek. *I* am getting divorced. Dodge the bullets, people.

Unconditional love is a great goal, but does it mean that you could marry *anybody*? Of course not! Because you are open-minded does it mean that *any* job would suit you? Of course not! Now, you could try to make both odd job and strange marriage work, and you might succeed to some extent, but I believe we are here to follow our bliss, as Joseph Campbell sagely directed us, and to find what *best* suits us, while dealing with those things which do not, as we wend our way down the Yellow Brick Road in the wisest way possible. We can have preferences without having to judge choices we do not select. We rely on discernment to take care of ourselves and our needs. So consider that I am being "discerning" when you might otherwise think that I am judging. And if I am out and out judging, contemplate that I'm doing it for fun and/or comedic effect and try not to get your knickers in a twist. I enjoy being outrageous! Play is one of the best ways to learn.

In these amazing times of planetary and personal transformation, it is imperative that we rely increasingly on our internal guidance system, our feelings, our intuition, our "gut." And yes, our *humanness*. I believe our humanness is the key to our enlightenment. We must go through, not around it to receive the gifts that are buried deep inside. In exploring ourselves, the good, bad, and ugly, we mine the gold. Gold dust can seem paltry at first, but after a couple hundred lifetimes, we start figuring out how to smelt the precious metal and turn it into nifty baubles and keepsakes.

I was raised a goody-two-shoes Theosophist among a group of them in New York City whose worst vice was being dull. Most were vegetarians, a couple of 'em smoked, none of 'em drank. Sex was not discussed though clearly we were not Shakers, as new Theosophists were occasionally spawned. There was even a sex scandal, but it was never openly discussed because Theosophists basked in the realm of ideas and ideals and avoided the Platform of the Personal like the plague.

This is where they lost me. Cause I'm a *person*. If there is no practical application of your philosophy to my life, if I don't *feel* better from learning its tenets, then it is of no use to me. I don't disagree with any of the Theosophical ideas. They were amazing for the time they came out (late 1800s) though the concepts themselves are timeless. But the presentation of the ideas did not evolve with the times. I'm not a Victorian. I'm a Valerie. Here and now. I've fought long and hard to achieve a state of raucous outrageousness, of irreverent liberation. It's why I curse. And drink. And have sex, when the wind blows in the right direction. It's why I'm here, and why I write. People need liberating from their own self-created prisons. I'm here to relate one escapee's way out.

Theosophy uses the construct of the Higher Self and *lower* self. I always resented it. 'Cause they were talking about *me* when they were referring to the lower self. My personality, my body, my inclinations, even my aspirations. (I wanted to sing, dance, and act). Me, *low*? And who was this Great Higher Self anyway? The Great and Powerful Oz? What makes *it* so special? Does it just keep me around to make it look good?

It was implicit that the personal human, the *ego*, was low, just like Christians were taught they were born sinners. We have derogatory associations with the word "low" just as we have elevated associations with "high." High Society, for instance, you low down dirty dog! I felt rather insulted as a small child and then later as a less small child. And what about my personal questions? What about sex? Love? (the very *conditional* kind). What of loss? Grief and pain? It was not discussed. It was left at "that's your karma." (What is? Teenaged curiosity about sex? The fact that no one talks about my Dad being dead?) Why is it okay for the Great Divine I Am to be the Great Divine I Am but *my* "I am" (that's all ego means, literally, in Greek) gets reduced to being some putz-y little psychological construct, abutted by a selfish id and a guilty superego? My puny, puffed-up self railed against the insult and indignity.

I don't know about you, but much as I love crystals and wind-catchers, silence and ritual, deep thoughts, introspection, meditation and revelation, there is much about spiritual and New Age teachings that just plain BORES me to death. Do I *really* need to read a book on *breathing*? I've been doing a pretty good job of it up to now (for the most part). I open some of these books and within a couple of sentences my eyes start to cross. Where's the sass? Where's the zip? The personality?

We are not here to transcend, but to *transmute* ourselves. Not rise above, but *take it with us and mix it with the other stuff.* That's all alchemy is. Taking the basic ingredients we came with: ego (check), insecurities (check), deadly sins, not so deadly sins, confusion, coercion, aspiration, inspiration, divination, mix it all together, have a couple hundred lifetimes, meditate a little, release a little, change a little, burp a little, et VOILA, enlightened person! Must I be relegated to a lifetime of filtered, room-temperature water and mung beans? (I drink filtered, room-temp water, by the way). Where's the wine, men, and song? Where's the chocolate? Where's the FUN, I ask? Have more fun. Joy is sacred. Angels fly because they take themselves so lightly.

To become enlightened people need to "En-lighten up" (to quote astute humorist Puppetji). We need to activate our CLOWN CHAKRA (to quote sagacious humorist Wavy Gravy). Just like Dharma Punx founder Noah Levine (a heavily tattooed, former convict), as I've grown more balanced, I like to keep my personality around for "flavah" and old time's sake. One doesn't have to shave one's' head and don orange robes to be deep. I can save the world in a bathing suit or my underwear, if I like. It's my party.

I'm a big advocate of speaking out about causes I feel passionate about, signing petitions, and sending emails to government officials and corporate heads. I am not a fan of marches and protests. We all have to find our comfort level, but doing something is *always* better than doing nothing. The key to this kind of work is keeping your cool and staying in your center. You do not have to be angry to be active. I know a lot of people eschew activism because they feel that focusing on what is wrong in this world creates more of what's wrong in the world. (Ye Olde Law of Attraction). I will grant you this. If you rant and rave and foam at the mouth, get no sleep, and are angry at the world, then their assertion is correct, you are contributing to the negativity on the planet. However, if, as I do, you have a glass of wine in hand, some jaunty music on in the background, and you are centered, confident, and happy when you take action, well, I say, there are lots of things that need fixing. Whistle while you work.

You can be a happy activist. I am. Sure, there are things that will get under my skin. (Animal abuse is a good one.) However, by speaking up and educating those who think that these egregious offenses (human and animal rights abuses, environmental destruction, poverty, disease, starvation, genocide, poisoning our water, bees, and food supply with GMOs, chemicals, and pesticides, shall I go on?) are okay, are, in fact, their way of conducting business and making profits, I say, no, you shall not continue unimpeded. The Dalai Lama speaks up, so does Thich Nhat Hanh. Bishop Desmond Tutu is an activist and so, obviously, was Nelson Mandela. Just because you're a man or woman of peace does not mean you don't get in the trenches. In fact, I feel it imperative that we do. How we define our goals is up to us. Meditating alone is not the answer.

My subjects veer between the sublime and the ridiculous. At times I get deadly serious. I don't skirt around the issues. Mine, at least. Now, who in *Heaven* am I? Read on, dear reader, read on…

CHAPTER 1

Make Me Happy

I love TED. For those who don't know what it is, rent the 2007 documentary *The Future We Will Create*. It showcases the mad genius flowing and gurgling out of our imagineers and visionaries. It made me proud to be human, here, now, and excited to see the future Planet Earth. We are AMAZING when we put our minds toward brilliance, art, science, healing, and community. I'm pretty sure the film featured the amazing computer technology that is now standard manual navigation for Apple's iPhones and iPads, so someone at Apple saw the TED demo and bought the software. Deals are made at the conference, plans are hatched, organizations are formed, worlds are changed. TED is a forum for artists and inventors, philosophers and candy makers alike. Willy Wonka would be an ideal speaker. Inspiration, childlike wonder, community, and connection is what TED is all about. Ancient Greece had Socrates babbling in the town square. We have TED.

Look up TED on YouTube and pick a speaker. The talks are 20 minutes and under. You'll find someone you'll like, most likely love, and possibly, someone who will inspire you to see things a new way. Try Sir Ken Robinson on education, for starters. I dare you not to be entranced.

I've never met a TED speaker (online, that is) I didn't like. Until a few nights ago. I was witnessing sheer heaven, award winning cinematographer Louie Schwartzberg's "Nature, Beauty, Gratitude." It's ten minutes. Go watch it online now. I'll wait for you.

After I watched, I saw a link for another TED talk, and I was intrigued by the saucy title: "F__k you. How to stop screwing yourself." Well, with an eye-catching title like that, especially spouted by a woman, how could I *not* look?

Mel Robbins is attractive, blonde, in good shape, and well dressed. She looks like the Republican version of author/speaker Elizabeth Gilbert, whose TED talks I liked well enough despite my not being an "Eat/Pray" fan. Mel is not just sure of herself, she is cocky. I have nothing against strong women. I am one. But this woman was a strident football coach. I adored Sandra Bullock's sassy wife/mom/mentor/rule-changing character in "The Blind Side," and Sally Field's "Norma Rae" (characters both based on real women), Eleanor Roosevelt, Gloria Steinem, Emma Goldman, Susan B. Anthony, Dorothy Parker, Mae West, even brassy Bella Abzug. I love women who buck the tide and challenge the status quo. That was not this woman. She was acerbic. Shrill. And tried way, *way* too hard to be cool, witty, and ugh, "likeable" (as evidenced by showing homey photos of her family). She even jumped off the stage into the audience in her heels to be "one of the people." Kiss of death.

I watched a few minutes then turned it off, but thought better of it the next day when I realized I could write about what she was ranting about. I "forced" myself to watch it—ironic when you find out that "forcing yourself to do things" is one of her prime tenets. Her philosophy runs directly counter to mine. But then, I don't have to *force* myself to do things. I'm an adult. I just do 'em.

I watched a full ten of her twenty minutes waiting for the moment when she would actually *say* something. Interesting. Provocative. TED-worthy. Eventually, her world-view became clear: "MAKE yourself do the crap you're supposed to do. FORCE yourself. Your mind prefers auto-drive, it likes to be comfortable, *you* like to be comfortable. FORCE yourself to be uncomfortable. As soon as you ''activate' yourself, your mind will fight and put on the emergency brake. Get out of your head! Get past your feelings! (past your feelings?! After I've worked so hard to get *into* my feelings?). You are never going to feel like doing it, so just do it. Be *honest* when people ask you how you are. You're not fine. You're either great or you're terrible. Which is it?"

Is she crazy? I have to give a full report to every passerby? People say "How are you" not because they want your actual update but because they are clumsily trying to say a simple "Hello," to acknowledge your presence. More people should just say, "Hi" and fewer people should say, "I'm *terrible*....whine, whine, whine," or "I'm great!...boast, boast, boast." Who has time for status reports?

I was exhausted just listening to her "Push! Push! Push!" agenda. I felt like I was in the labor and delivery wing. She was saying we couldn't trust ourselves. Our natural selves. She was calling us shiftless and lazy. I happen to disagree. When they panned the audience, I saw more than one person with their arms crossed (body language for "just say no"). I've scanned her blog and webpage, and I'm *not* wanting more. What I want to talk about is why.

Mel's credentials are listed as "a married, working mother of three, an ivy educated, criminal lawyer, and one of the top career and relationship experts in America." She has book, radio and TV shows, and a column in *Success Magazine*. Of course. Everything about her *screams* success. "Most nights, once the kids are in bed, you'll find Mel at home with a bourbon on the rocks and her Australian Shepherd at her feet, writing about life, love, and everything else on her award-winning blog." Blecch.

This is exactly why people like me (not married, no kids, no searing career, blah, blah, blah) get DEPRESSED. I'm supposed to be like her —bourbon, shepherd, and children in tow? Why is that the gold standard? It doesn't make her a success. It makes her married with kids and lots of jobs. It makes her *busy*. In many ways, I think it's what's wrong with the American dream, and the American work ethic. Bigger, better, faster, more, no, MORE! Busy, busy, push, push. No one takes the time to just BE. We are human be-ings. Not human do-ings. People have no idea how to sit still. I think we've incurred ADHD with our behaviors, our need for speed, and our addiction to rapid-fire media missives.

Just because you're accomplished doesn't mean you're happy. People pushpushpush while on autopilot and neglect to ask themselves if they enjoy what they're doing. Mel complained about people who aren't satisfied and implied that they're not go-getters, but lazy and complacent. Well, say I, what of go-getters who are not satisfied? Are they happy, or just *busy*? They are doing what they think they should (aren't all women supposed to be married with kids AND huge media stars with multiple book and TV deals?). Egads. Why is this even a goal? Because of the money? The fame? *American Idol* is not my idol. We know fame and fortune don't grant happiness. Happiness is a state of *mind*, not a state of affairs. Besides, comedian Stephen Wright was right when he said, "You can't have it all. Where would you put it?"

Another thing that drives me nuts is when inspirational speakers say, "If I can do it, you can do it." What do you have to do with me? Seriously. I may be inspired by your story but your success most assuredly does not guarantee mine. My success (or lack thereof) will not look like yours when I achieve it. What we need are gems of inspiration that we can take and make our own.

I went to an ivy-league college. I wasn't happy there and I'm not blaming the school. I take responsibility for how I feel. We have the power, with our attitude, to have a great or terrible time. And if something really, truly is terrible (or seems terrible) because it is a bad fit for you, it is still teaching you about what you DO want by showing you what you DON'T want. This is how we learn, and there's the gift. It's an if-then thing. If not this, then that...if not that, then something else. It's trial and... *learning*. There is no right or wrong. Only what works.

If you don't like something, change it. If you can't change it, change your attitude. And if something just plain old sucks lemons and you're not in the mood to make lemonade, well, that's okay, too. We're all entitled to our moods, so long as we don't unleash them unkindly on others. Lick your wounds in private, don't take it out on the dog or your kids. Or on yourself, for that matter. People punish themselves all the time, jumping out of the frying pan into the fire. Be brave and sit it out. Have faith that you have the strength and fortitude to get through whatever it is, and that you will take some sound experience and wisdom along with you when you get past the bumpy stuff.

I had pushpushpush the first half of my life from a mother who pushpushpushed me. Made me a nervous wreck. Yes, I did well in school. But I didn't like to hear the clock ticking and feel someone breathing down my back. I've had to UN-learn that stressful, type-A, anxiety-filled way of living. So what works for me? Taking full breaths and realizing I have control in my life. I don't have to *push*. I don't have to *run*. And here's a big one: I don't have to do things I don't want to do. I don't have to suffer. *Conversations with God* by Neale Donald Walsch said it thus, "A master feels pain, but she does not suffer." Pain is a physical sensation. Suffering is a state of mind. We hold reign over that kingdom when we examine and change our beliefs. Even if your pain is emotional, you don't have to compound it by judging or bemoaning the hurt. Feel it, understand it, and process it. So it may take more than two weeks. You can do it. You're worth it.

Some people are happy to be unhappy and make excuses when you (I mean me) make suggestions as to how to make something better, or make it go away. ("But I can't stop, I *have* to do it, put up with it, stick with it," etc.) Author/New Age guru Louise Hay learned to back off when giving advice as soon as she heard the words "Yeah, but…" If someone is gonna "yeah, but" you, they don't want to change. They just want to complain. When someone really wants to learn a different way, they'll listen. And they'll make the changes they need to make to alter their lives. We all have that ability. But we have to want it. The magic key is to get in touch with our *wanting,* with our desire. To coax with a carrot (or carat) and not traumatize with threats of inadequacy and failure. There is a *huge* difference between the two approaches, indeed, a world of difference. One is a gorgeous, gloppy, three-tiered chocolate cake. The other is mucking out the barn. When desire is generated organically ("Did you say that cake was CALORIE FREE?" "Why yes! Yes, I did!" I chime back), we initiate our very own gold rush.

Mel went on in her lecture, "I will do whatever it takes to make you do what you have to do." Direct quote? No. I couldn't bear to listen to her a third time. But I'm nearly positive that's the sentiment she was expressing, life coach that she is (and if she isn't, she might as well be). That sentiment implies that she is responsible for our progress and success. Don't you believe her or teachers like her. You get the credit, and no one else, for what you do, even if someone "helped" you. There's only one person who can do the work in life, in *your* life, and that's you. Yeah, sure, go to a therapist or a coach. You could also talk to a friend. Talk to yourself. Talk to God. Journal. Take a hike. Go for a swim. When we still our minds and calm our emotions, that's when we receive inspiration from the deepest, highest part of who we are. We all have a Guru. She's living inside our hearts. All we have to do is activate our heart centers. Rev those engines and zoom off in a blaze of love and glory.

The clearest route to access this wisdom within is to listen to our feelings. This I believe from the bottom of my heart...we must trust our feelings. We've been trained against them, favoring instead the rational. Nah-ah. *All wrong.* We have feelings *and* thoughts for a reason. So they can work in concert. Think with your heart. Feel with your head. Feelings are the language of the soul. We need *more* soul in our lives. Not more push-pushpush. When we get in the flow with ourselves, in sync with our selves, guess what happens? Synchronicity. Enchantment. Magic. Happy coincidences. Serendipity. We attune to the forces within. "May the force be with you" is not something you can coerce. You can't force "the force." It's a Zen thing. It's gotta flow organically. One must allow it. Will it to come. Invite. Intend it. Receive. But a football coach sure ain't gonna scream inspiration out of you.

I gentle myself. I don't want a jarring alarm in the morning, I wake up naturally, but there are gentle alerts these days for those that need them, including Zen chimes. I had a most remarkable experience one morning when someone woke me to the music of Harry Nilsson's "Everybody's Talkin," the beautiful theme song from "Midnight Cowboy." I never knew you could start your day with song. That morning changed my life. Gentle yourself through life.

Remember the scene in *The Blind Side* when Sandra speaks the magic words that *inspire* her son to play football like never before? Inspire means to "breathe in," to take in the "force," or prana (divine light or life force) naturally. That's what lungs do. You have to *relax* to allow them to expand fully. She inspires him to *think* of his teammates as her family (which is his new family), how they have his back, and he theirs. She motivates him with a *thought* that touches his heart, and it is that fire, that passion, that ignites his will, his energy, his "force," and yes, his *feelings*. But in fact, he is the one that initiates the ignition sequence. If he didn't comprehend what she said, if he didn't *agree*, it wouldn't have worked. So, in fact, and this is very, *very* important, HE INSPIRED HIMSELF. He motivated himself. No one does it for you.

Jesus said, "You can plant seeds on rock, but they won't take root." We are the ones who decide whether we are fertile ground or barren rock. No one inspires us. No one *makes* us happy. No one makes us sad. We are our own marching band, coach, inspiration, or desperation. And when you realize that, boy, are you powerful. This is not to negate the power of love, support, and insight we receive from friends, loved ones, strangers, and yes, coaches. We are not alone. But we alone are responsible for our state of mind and the feelings those thoughts and beliefs engender.

Sure, you can have a down day. I do. Have sour thoughts. I indulge them when I'm grumpy. Some people even have bad decades. I'm no sugarcoated Pollyanna. But we have the resilience to pull *out* of these moods. This is the greatest power the human has. Resilience. The ability to recover. The ability to survive wars and holocausts and move past them to *thrive*. Some stay rooted in misery and relive the past and their pains. Others move on. What's the difference? Their mental software. Make sure you're running an operating system that supports your happiness.

Your thoughts and feelings are your creation. If you don't like what you're experiencing, look at how you're programming your day. "I love myself. I trust life. I believe in love. My life is getting better and better every day. I trust myself. I am love. I am loved. I am wonderful. I am okay. Everything is okay. Everything is going to be okay." Do those words resonate? Do they agree with you? Great! If not—okay. Find words that do. Write your own mantras. Better that than your epitaph.

"I hate my life. I hate myself. I hate my body. I hate my job. I hate my home. I hate my spouse. I hate the government. I hate the terrorists. I hate the weather. I hate." How did *those* words "make" you feel? Did they uplift? Make you nervous? Resonate? Make you realize you need a new job? There's no reason to suffer. But the words themselves have no power. Their meaning is different for all of us (for no two of us feel and think the same thing) and strikes different chords of resonance with different people, or no resonance at all. They are just words. But when they do have resonance for you, choose carefully. What you think creates how you feel and determines how you live and what you will experience. If, then…Cause and effect. Plant a seed, grow a flower. Or a pickle.

So, no thank you, Mel. I don't want your "tough-love" scaring me to get out of my "comfort zone." I've worked too hard for too long to get *into* my comfort zone. I want to be happy. I want to be comfortable in my own skin. I *want* to trust myself. Life can be effortless and easy, that is, in fact, the way God designed it to be (She and I are tight). "Be ye as the lilies in the field. They neither spin nor toil." (I'll switch that out to "strive nor toil." Spinning is not a *real* big problem nowadays).

When we "follow our bliss," as Joseph Campbell directs us, when we *trust* our wants and listen to our feelings, they will warn us against people, places, and things. They will incline us *toward* other people, places, and things that resonate with who we are and what we want. The big, subtle twist is this: Move toward your wants, not away from your "not-wants." Attraction vs. repulsion. Honey vs. vinegar. Use desire for your goals as your motivation, not distaste for what you no longer want. The difference is huge, and practical. When you start fueling your life with desire, magic unfurls.

When we create comfort for ourselves, we get in *alignment* with who we really are. We are God. We are love incarnate. God is Love and Joy. Therefore, at our core, we are Love and Joy. Our job is to jackhammer off all the dried muck that we've allowed to cake onto our juicy, golden soul. "All this and more ye can do," said Jesus. We (I'm talking about you and me!) are amazing creators and imagineers, not just the TED talkers. We are creating a Beautiful New World. If we allow it. Believe it. Activate it. Will it. Now *that*? *That* "makes" me happy.

CHAPTER 2

Making Peace

I was older than most when I entered the world of sexual activity, and I was still relatively new to the field of dating when I met this guy. I was an actress at a theatre company in the West Village, and he was there videotaping a friend's show that night. I felt a striking jolt of electricity hit my solar plexus when I laid eyes on him. He was gorgeous, with healthy, golden, athletic good looks. I was short, perky, and quirky. He responded to my flirting and we went to a party together that night. I was mesmerized by his looks, but ultimately became bored by his total self-involvement and seeming lack of interest in me. He drank beer after beer as he rambled on about Scorsese, De Niro, and *Raging Bull*, the ultimate guy movie. He stared off into space, never even glancing at me. My excitement that he was talking to me eventually faded into ennui. The electric buzz was gone. My feet hurt from standing in the small, ugly, fluorescently lit kitchen so I departed to sit in the living room. When I eventually glimpsed him again in the kitchen, that same strange jolt of electricity hit my solar plexus. This had never happened to me before, and hasn't happened since. It was a message from Spirit saying "Karma alert. Pay attention." I paid attention, all right.

I loitered as long as I possibly could until boredom overwhelmed me again. I wished him a good night. It was at that point that he expressed his first direct interest in me. "Where are you going?" It was three in the morning, raining, I was in the Lower East Side, and he had a car. He offered to drive me home. He was to become my first-acknowledged, one night stand. And my husband.

My parents died when I was young, and there was nothing I wanted more in the world than to get married, have children, and act. But I was so morbidly depressed at 22 when my second parent died that I barely had a pulse. I decided to lose my virginity at 24 one Friday night when I had nothing better to do. It came in the form of room service. This guy I knew from growing up in my apartment building rang my doorbell one night and that was that. He liked *Raging Bull*, too. I got my knickers in a twist over him though we only slept together a handful of times. Brief, casual flings with two other guys ensued, breaking my heart each and every time. I was a novice. Growing up without a father or brothers and having a mother who never dated left me without the most basic of skills with the opposite sex. I was desperate for action and petrified simultaneously. By the time I met the guy at the theatre, I said, "Aha! I get it! This is just sex! " Boy, was I wrong.

He had all the confidence that I lacked. He was cocky, rude even, and that bravado appealed to my worn-and-torn ego. I wasn't confident. I was pudgy and sexually inexperienced. I had one sister who I didn't get along with and rarely saw. This guy was from a large Catholic family, with four siblings and myriad nieces and nephews. His parents were young, vibrant, fun, and they loved me. I was a good girl. Despite his wild nature, he verbally indicated that he was serious about me, and that marriage was down the road. This made me very happy. He was gorgeous, vibrant, and he was mine.

Except that he wasn't. He wasn't particularly devoted to me, or loyal, or caring. He always did his own thing, and never, ever referred to "us." The word "we" was not in his vocabulary. It was always "*I'm* going out, *I'm* doing this" Me. Me. Me. "I'll see you when I look at you," was a favorite phrase of his. I was constantly off-kilter, insecure, and felt like a hanger on. I *was* a hanger on. He had other girls hanging on, too, new ones, and old ones. I wished he would push them away but he never did. I certainly wasn't going to do it for him. I wanted him to *want* to do it out of love and loyalty to me, to us. Never happened. After we were married, I heard him consoling a young fling from Colorado he'd had three years prior on the phone. "It wasn't you...It was me."

I was livid that he was offering any kind of consolation to some bimbo when he offered little or none to me, his wife, with my dead parents and all.

I kept hoping he would mature and grow to appreciate what he had, but he never did. Instead, he got worse. We both took care of him, and neither of us took care of me. I decided to pull back to see if he would step up to the plate. Nope. I know he loved me. He just didn't do anything about it. His love was entirely theoretical. I was exhausted from being neglected, and my anger grew so great that my entire body literally turned lobster red one day when he showed up 45 minutes late for our first (and last) one-hour marriage counseling session.

By the time he left I was relieved, but he also owed me a lot of money since I had subsidized our life together, and had set him up in the business of his dreams. He paid me back very, very slowly, contrary to our very specific legal repayment schedule. In the meantime, he amassed an empire of sorts, and a nineteen year old girlfriend to boot, an oil heiress, or so I heard. He paid me back partially, remaining in arrears for years, as he claimed he didn't have the money to pay me back. This was because he had acquired a loft in Tribeca, vintage furniture, and was growing his business. She had a condo in the East Village, and together they had a country house upstate. It was all just too fabulous. I couldn't understand why things were going so, *so* well for him, and not, seemingly, so for me. I was stuck in a big fat rut of resentment.

The years ticked by and I was still single. But I had started to change, to date, to live, to lose weight, get in shape, perform, write, work, and generally gain confidence in myself. I was living my life in ways I never had before. Ten years went by and I wondered if I would ever see the person I had loved and hated so much. It wasn't a burning desire, more of an idle curiosity. He had entered my life with a jolt of electricity and left while I was soot-covered and smoldering.

Years later I was recovering from another unstable relationship and was *convinced* (I now know this was a psychic impression leading me to my destiny that night) that I would find the fellow in Central Park, back together with his old girlfriend. I had been exercising all day in various forms, my best stress reliever. By the time I put my blades on and got to Central Park to find him, it was obvious I had no more energy left. So instead of doing the full loop, which I normally do, I decided to call it quits at the 72nd Street Band Shell.

There was my ex-husband. He was playing Frisbee with his old friends, the people I had socialized with for six years. All my anxiety over the recent guy I was strung out over dissipated. Of all the shocking reactions I could have had, I was surprised to find myself suddenly filled with the greatest love for my ex. There he was, older, fatter, and covered with facial hair. He wasn't pretty anymore. He looked like the grizzled mountain man from Colorado he'd driven out East with. I felt all the love I had ever felt for him, and despite hating Frisbee with a passion when I was with him (cause he played it every frickin' day), all I could think was, wow, here he is, playing Frisbee, isn't that wonderful? It was a beatific moment. I was basking in love, for him, and myself. I was proud of my body, my sexuality, and my life. I had come such a long, long way. I sat on a bench ten feet away and observed while he played. I basked in amazement at this astonishing encounter. I was filled with an indescribable peace.

He didn't notice me. He was mid-toss when I finally called out his name. He didn't hear me. I shouted it louder. He *couldn't* hear me. My voice had been erased from his data bank. I shouted louder one last time. He looked over at me with a totally blank expression, with no recognition whatsoever, as if I were a stranger. Or a ghost. I smiled, waved my hand at him, and said, "Person you were married to?" He continued to stare blankly. I said, "Can you talk?"

He finally spoke. "Can you wait?" And he finished out his game.

This was exactly how he treated me when we were together. Kept me waiting, put me second, no third, to whatever else was going on in his life. But now, instead of being hurt by it, I found it to be *hilarious*! No, it was FANTASTIC. I felt even *more* love for him! I finally understood. This is simply who he is—a totally self-absorbed guy who likes to play Frisbee. When I was with him I figured he treated me that way because I wasn't cute or sexy enough, he didn't love me enough, he wasn't *in* love with me. If I was *cuter* (the self-hating voice went), he would drop the disc and rush to be at his beloved's side. But now I could see the truth. He's just fucking rude. I was smiling so hard I almost collapsed to the ground with giddiness. This was liberation, V-Day from my own miserable war with myself.

I waited what felt like twenty minutes for his "jam" to finish (there were no points, mind you, he was just tossing the disc with someone he plays with all the time). It had been ten years since I'd seen him. What was another few minutes? I continued to brim with love as I witnessed this activity that had been *so* anathema to me when we were together.

His mother had defended his obsession. "At least, he's not with another woman."

I responded, "He might as well be with another woman for all the time and attention I get from him. What's the difference?"

I said perfunctory hellos to the Frisbee crowd, but I wasn't there for niceties. Everybody left. The sun was setting and we sat on a bench 'til it was pitch dark out. I excitedly grilled him on every aspect of his life, about his girlfriend of nine years, now an old woman of 28. Did he want to have kids with her, marry her some day? Yes, he did. I felt no jealousy or discomfort. In fact, I was *grateful* that he was with someone else. It meant he wasn't torturing me! I asked about everyone in his large family. They were all alive and thriving. I was genuinely happy for him. Happy he was in a relationship, and *particularly* happy he was fat (since he had warned me when we were married, "If you ever get fat, I'll divorce you").

I thanked him for everything, for being the brother I never had, for teaching me how to drink beer, live life bigger, harder, and wilder. He was a bad boy and in being with him I had loosened up. In fact, I was so tightly wound when I met him, I needed to learn how to be more selfish. I sat at the feet of a master. He had informed my artistic sensibility, for he loved alternative music and the downtown performance art scene. We saw John Leguizamo, Eric Bogosian, and other avant-garde shows. He expanded my horizons. I thanked him for it all. He thanked me for giving him New York, said it was "intoxicating." At no point did he ask me anything about myself, my life, or my only relative. He did not comment on how good I looked. I kept smiling, kept on loving him, finally accepting him *as is*. *Getting* what he is. Crappy to be married to. Not so bad on a park bench for an hour. I had no expectations or desire to be loved by him now. We hugged, and he teared up.

"Leaving you was the hardest thing I ever did in my entire life," he said. "You being all alone in the world and all."

I burst into a broad smile, just short of a laugh. This pathos was hilarious. Was it some form of guilt? He was banging some blonde broad before, during, and after he left me. He even brought her into my home, breaching our agreement that neither of us would do so while we were still living together, and left evidence out for me to find. He was so busy having fun with her that he neglected to find a new apartment, and when he did, he asked me to put my name on his lease "to help him out." (I declined.) He stayed in my home and bed an additional five weeks, which was excruciatingly painful for me.

I smiled and punched him gently in the arm as I responded, "You made it look *real* easy."

Finally, he said quietly, "You look good."

He then asked (very tentatively) if I was seeing anyone. It seemed he was afraid to hear the answers. Did he think I would turn into jelly when he left? I was *livid* when our relationship ended, not sad. That anger fueled my new life. I had conquered many worlds since his departure. I wasn't yet a writer when we were together. Since then I'd co-written a screenplay, written a couple of TV pilots by myself, and was scripting and performing my own solo stage shows. Things had changed. Was I performing, he inquired? Yes, I was. A solo show I had written. I was amazed he asked me anything. We hugged. He sniffled. I was glowing like Mother Mary. I didn't *need* anything from him anymore. I was free.

I rollerbladed home in the dark of Central Park, moving fierce and fast. Yes, it was like seeing a ghost. Seeing him cry and hearing him say that leaving me was hard was sorta-kinda like saying he had loved me. Who knew? I guess I didn't really feel it when we were a couple. When I got home, I drank the rest of a bottle of white wine and lay down on the floor, sobbing.

He came to see my one-woman show, a piece about sex and dating. My producer was very curious to see what he looked like and was shocked when he came in wearing a long coat and some sort of black hat. I suppose he thought he looked fashionably downtown.

She thought he looked like an Orthodox Jew and said, "I can't see you with him."

"I wasn't," I said. "I was with a cute, young Irish guy."

When she commented that he looked like a fire plug, I was stupefied. Early on in our relationship, he and I went on a double date on a very snowy night. He walked ahead with our friends and left me shuffling in the snow, like a Geisha, six feet behind. I asked him why he wouldn't walk with me and he said, "You look like a fire hydrant."

(I'm short and, apparently, my winter bundling created the impression that I was a fireman and dog's best friend). I had a high threshold for pain and was so desperate to belong, to be loved, that I (metaphorically) took it up the ass from him. When my producer called him a fire plug I had never heard a more exact, full circle rendition of "what goes around comes around."

He drank a can of beer out of a rumpled brown paper bag during my show like a common drunk, and, when it was over, he said, "You were okay," and lumbered out.

That was it. I looked after him incredulously and called his name. I lifted my arms up as if to say, "That's it?"

He came back, hugged me stiffly, said, "I have to go," and was gone.

I cried because it was so cold, so mean, and so, well, *him*.

After the audience left the small theatre, my producer listened while I cried and tried to fathom what had just happened. Why did he bother coming to my show? Why did he bother marrying me? None of it made sense. It was unsettling, disheartening, and dispiriting. Just like our marriage. I had been in it alone, playing house all by myself.

I don't rue this relationship. I believe it was meant to be. As one channeled message said to me, "Not all lessons in love are learned through love. Don't doubt the rightness of this relationship. You both scripted it before you were born." As surely as I felt that jolt of electricity when I first laid eyes on him, he had his own otherworldly experience the night we met. He later admitted that when I jumped on stage after the play he was videotaping was over, he heard a voice inside his head, "You're going to marry that girl."

When I asked him what he thought of me that night he paused then said, "I thought your jeans were too tight," which I realized later was code for, "I thought you were fat."

I guess he needed the psychic kick in the pants to fulfill his karmic debt to the fat girl. When I sought channeled guidance after the marriage had ended, the energies told me I wasn't really mad at him (you coulda fooled me!). They said, "You are mad at yourself. You put *his* wants before your *needs*."

Bingo. We both catered to him, we both ignored me. Mea culpa.

But I knew something now that I didn't know then when I was wearing Laura Ashley and trying to be the perfect housewife. It wasn't that I wasn't sexy enough or cool enough or smart or adventurous enough that he didn't love me passionately. He didn't love me well because *he just doesn't love well*. It was him. It never was me.

Years ago I went to a very colorful psychic in the West Village who chain smoked brown cigarettes. As I ascended the stairs to his smoke filled lair he asked, "What do you do?"

I thought he was supposed to tell *me* things. I felt like saying, "I'm a secretary," because that was my job but as I huffed and puffed up the stairs to his aerie, I muttered quietly, "I'm an actress."

"Of course you are! Your aura is lavender! You live alone?"

I was situated across from him now, his desk between us. "Yes," I replied, annoyed that I was paying him to play twenty questions and that I was providing all the answers. "*Yes*, I live alone."

"Of course you do! And you wear your independence like a tiara!" The guy looked like Nathan Lane and sounded like P.T. Barnum. He was a showman, with gold hoop earrings going up and down both ears, a gay pirate with a gorgeous husband downstairs. "Have you ever been married?"

For the love of God, was he ever going to tell *me* anything? "*Yes*, I've been married."

He was offended. "What made you think you could be married?"

Now I was offended! I keep a nice home, I'm a good cook, I like to have fun in the sack and elsewhere, what's the fucking problem?

"You're an artist. You're not a domestic type."

Oh, lord. Couldn't I be both? He depressed me further by seeing a future mate. Short, with dark curly hair, glasses, younger than me. This was not my dream man by a stretch. I didn't want to be with another kid. But, in fact, this vision was accurate. Dark, curly hair with glasses was the exact guy I was strung out on when I bumped into my ex. He was never marriage material. But the psychic saw him clearly.

Years later, I found out that my ex and his girlfriend had a baby. I bumped into two of his Frisbee friends and they blurted the news to me casually, assuming I knew, then looked at each other, worried (like Beavis and Butthead), when they realized I didn't. Uh, oh. What would she do? Would she freak out? Would she break down? I could hardly contain my laughter. He who fancied himself a downtown artiste was now a suburban dad, something he had snickered at when others had succumbed to that lifestyle, the very lifestyle I coveted.

No, this...*this* was amusing. He and I had switched brains when we were married just as surely as Gene Wilder and Peter Boyle had in *Young Frankenstein*. He was changing diapers, and I was reveling in my life, a downtown, solo-performance artist. That had been his dream, not mine. Through my anger and pain I had forged ahead and created a life of, for, and by myself. No partner. No baby. No new homes. No family to fall back on. I stood alone in my spotlight.

CHAPTER 3

Lean On Me

These are the best of times. These are the worst of times. Horns are honking out my city window, the bells, whistles, and howls of a convoy of fire trucks and god knows who and what else. But despite the sometimes seemingly endless chaos of 3D life, spiritual light is increasing daily and affecting us physically, emotionally, mentally, and spiritually. We may feel tired, and have aches, allergies, and pains as we release the past and open ourselves to love and light. Often I am exhausted, at other times exhilarated.

We are absorbing the new energies of the Golden Age in time-release fashion, so we don't blow our circuits. Spirit is marinating us so that we can physically hold more of our soul's light. Not everyone is receptive to this change, to the promise of a new world, but change is inevitable. Growth, however, is optional. While planetary peace, joy, and light palpably grow, chaos and confusion still abound for some as the dark house of cards falls. There are more homeless people on the streets of New York City than I've seen in ages. A few weeks ago,

I counted eight people begging within the span of a quarter of a city block.

Despite the spiritual joy that I stand confidently in now, I've never denied my humanity, sadness, depression, or anger. You can only move through those emotions by owning, looking at, and learning from them. I used to feel great then fall into an abyss of self-doubt and recrimination ("recrimination" looks a lot like re-criminalizing yourself, doesn't it?). I sulked and soaked in a murky bath of low self-esteem with occasional bouts of joy and celebration.

About a year ago I was not feeling as consistently exhilarated as I do now. I was choosing to feel frustrated about the scraggly state of my love life and career. A friend suggested, "Maybe you need your career to be on track before anything happens with your love life?"

"Aaargh," I replied.

Why must there be a prerequisite? I didn't cotton to the idea of having to pass yet more tests to get where I wanted to go, I already felt like a circus dog, jumping through endless rings of fire as I worked on issue after personal issue over the decades. Or was it centuries?

I was on my way to an audition for a TV gig with such an insipid script I didn't even care about getting the job. Until I got there. The audition was in an upscale studio, a light, bright, professional space that smelled of success, money, and sophistication. I may not like bad TV (and yes, there is good TV) but I do like money. In fact, I love it. Money is energy, pure and simple, and means nothing until you transform it with a transaction. There is nothing unspiritual about money. Everything is a physical manifestation of spirit. It's what you do with it that matters.

I knew the woman holding the audition (she wrote the script). She had a bouncy personality, was beautiful, married with kids, had a house and her own business. Nothing was missing (except a good script). "Why can't I be like her?" I wondered. "Why have the outward trappings of a husband, family, and success eluded me?" I silently moaned. "Because I'm a New Age Alien, that's why." Because I'm a loner and a mystic. I like solitude. I want a partner who likes quiet and solitude, too, as well as a rousing good time (with me, that is. I had a husband who liked a rousing good time with other people. Not so fun for me). Since I proudly live in a TV-free home, trying to get a job in TV created a disconnect. I felt like a perpetual outsider, always running up the down staircase. My performing talents were not destined for mass media. I recriminated myself for not being what I wanted. I recriminated myself for being myself.

As I descended the stairs to the hot, smelly subway I walked past an Archie Bunker type served up with an extra side of old and fat. Burdened by the heat and his weight, he lumbered like a gorilla on the crowded platform, slowly bucking the tide of rushing people. I stopped and stared as he walked past me, intrigued by his plodding stride in the midst of bustling crowds. What was his story? Was he sick? Homeless? He sported a pink baseball cap that read, "PRINCESS," that he must have found somewhere. I felt humbled. I wasn't the only non-success in this city. On the other hand, maybe he did buy it. This is New York.

I glumly got on the crowded E train, dragging my feet to this audition that required a reasonable level of perkiness. How was I gonna pull that off? How did other actors turn on the "happy" vibe and book jobs? It beat the hell out of me, and, as a result, I never managed to nab a commercial career. As I moved to sit on the crowded subway car, an exhausted Latina woman to my left pulled her purse in to accommodate my ass. Looming over me was a tall, young, attractive, athletic black man. His leg was injured. He leaned on a single crutch and held a wrapped sandwich in his free hand. I offered him my seat. He smiled and declined.

I was already starting to feel better. The simple act of offering him my seat connected us. I pulled out my trusty New Age *Sedona Journal of Emergence* and started to read. The exhausted lady to my left started to lean imperceptibly, then more dramatically toward me as she fell asleep. Why couldn't she fall the other way, on the metal seat rail? She could comfortably (well, maybe not so comfortably) sleep without troubling *it*. But no, her semiconscious body sought out a cozy compadre, albeit a stranger. I squirmed away from her and she responded by lethargically straightening up.

A young black woman across the aisle watched our antics, the white girl, comically squirming away from the sleeping Latina. The guy with the crutch had taken a seat to my right. I felt we were friends, he and I, and when sleeping beauty slumped toward me, I squirmed toward him for safety, resting my head briefly on his shoulder for comedic effect. My depression was now gone. I had playfully engaged myself in this vignette. I loved New York, and myself, for subtly bringing four strangers together in this spontaneous silent movie.

The girl across the aisle was smiling now. Perhaps my target audience was on the subway? An aroma of liquor began to waft over from sleeping beauty. When she looked ready to totally pass out on me, I jerked away, pulling the rug out from beneath her. I'm nice, but I'm not a futon. She jolted awake.

Her eyes came into focus as she took me in. I smiled. This calmed her. "I was dreaming of my husband," she said.

I thought it strange that she shared something so intimate with me. "That's nice," I responded. I hadn't written her off as a lunatic. Yet.

"It was nice," she said. With a dreamy, faraway look she continued, "I have a husband." Uh huh. "And two boyfriends." Well, that explained it.

"No wonder you're so tired!" I exclaimed. "You're very busy."

"After forty, you *gotta* stay busy," she responded. Silence, then she continued, "My husband left me."

"Oh," I said. We'd shifted from comedy to tragedy.

She sat up abruptly. "Did we pass Seventh Avenue?" she blurted.

"Yes," I answered.

"That was my stop."

"Oh," I said again. A pause.

She smiled wryly and said, "You're nice."

The hung-over, drunk-ish woman who missed her husband and her stop, and the depressed, lonely actress with no joie de vivre that morning bonded. Forty-Second Street was coming up, two stops past her intended destination. "Are you getting off here?" I asked.

She nodded and started to get up. I touched her arm and, feeling she needed the comfort, gently stroked her back.

This leaning tower of sleep kissed her fingers then crossed herself. She looked at me with sad, sweet eyes. "God Bless You."

And so my depressed foray into the humid gray day wasn't for naught. Perhaps I am the patron saint of such people. In a city full of "winners," the too-rich-too-drugged-too-desperate, busy, needy, neurotic, over-sexed, greedy, self-indulgent narcissists who notice nothing but Gucci ads, I notice those with crutches, empty bottles, and lost looks. I live in both worlds, being both enfranchised (I have a home, clothes, and food) and lost (Who the hell am I? What am I doing here?).

As I exited the subway I passed a homeless black guy sitting on the sidewalk in the intense, early-morning heat. He was slumped, dozing against a brick wall. It was impossible to miss the large print on his tee-shirt, "FUTURE TROPHY WIFE." He is the long lost cousin of "PRINCESS," the unrecognized royalty of this city.

I know that my service as a performer and a writer is to light up the world with emotion, with humor, with compassion, with bravado, and with humility. It's not for network TV or the big screen. But I shine my light every day. Even in the subway. Maybe especially in the subway, where it's needed most.

I know who I am. I know what I am. I know why I'm here. I know how I serve. I am love incarnate. I am the word of God. I am the hands and feet of the divine. I am the infinite power and presence of the divine. We all are. It is imperative that we act, be and feel from this knowing. Om. Peace.

CHAPTER 4

How To Give A Bad Psychic Reading

You're frustrated with your life. Bored out of your mind. You hate your job, hate your spouse, your apartment, your socks, possibly even your eyebrows. Your clothes don't fit, your hair has seen better days, and well...*well*...you just need some *help*. You have a therapist, you go to the gym, but you want someone, someone with the weight of "mirror, mirror" wisdom, to tell you, *It's all going to be okay.* That's all we really want to know, right? That it all ends "happily ever after?" However, until the end, there are myriad plot twists and turns we have to get through until we reach the white picket fence, or whatever it is we want. Even then, the fence will need repairing or replacing, won't it? As Roseanne Roseannadanna said, "It's always *something*."

We imagine that when we get what we want (I am guilty of this) that all our problems will be over. What happens when you get what you want? You get a whole *new* set of problems. They may even cost you more (Lear Jets are *not* cheap. And where are you going to park it? You have to keep the pilot happy...the list goes on). How do you *know* if you have problems? Easy. If you're still breathing.

Now, problems are not necessarily a bad thing. Think of them as brainteasers. Something to keep us busy while we're breathing. But since we like to solve problems like dogs like to chew bones, we seek gratification after the brain tickling. We go to the gym to get results. We go to psychics for answers. It's a wee, teeny bit of cheating, wanting to read the last page in the book before you're into the third chapter. We hope our prognosticator has access to the Cliff Notes version of our life.

I'm all about internal guidance and trusting yourself. You are the authority on you, no one else. Our society leads us away from trusting our nature, our feelings, thoughts, and inclinations. And we've picked up some crappy habits over the millennia, giving our power away to corporations, the church, and governments. 2012 marked the shift away from disempowerment to the empowerment of We The People.

Even with confidence in my own intuition, from time to time I want to hear a tangible answer from the universe. I mean, a psychic. Now, I am psychic, and so are you (we all have ways and means to discern what we need to know) but we are not able to glean everything about our life. In fact, we're not meant to. If we knew the play by play the day we were born, what fun would there be in living it?

We come to earth with a blueprint designed by us and our spirit advisors before birth. We sign off on the basics. That's what a blueprint is, a foundation. We agree to the major probabilities that will provide us with lessons we need to learn this round on the cosmic carrousel. We fill in the blanks (that part's called free will). In a way, our lives are like coloring books. The outlines are blocked out, but we select the colors and the medium. Do we want pencils, crayons, or paint? Up to us. The big plot points are set in stone. We get to do the decorating. Will our lives be dull gray or a vibrant watercolor? You could look at it like planning a vacation (do you want Patagonia, St. Bart's, Paris, or a fat farm?) or like selecting classes and a major in college. Once you matriculate, will you coast and cut class or go for Phi Beta Kappa? As we carve our characters with the choices we make, I think it's possible some of our major plot points may shift. They may become easier. Or just seem easier if we assume a more useful attitude. Do we approach the river of life kicking and screaming or do we flow with the current?

If you haven't seen it yet rent *Defending Your Life* starring Meryl Streep and Albert Brooks. It's one of the funniest and clearest depictions of life purpose and destiny out there. Also, the books *Journey of Souls* and *Destiny of Souls* by Michael Newton very clearly elucidate these points with case histories of patients he hypnotized and regressed to the pre-birth state of consciousness.

So we meet with our guides before incarnating and plot out a coupla traumas here, a nice love affair there, a possible exit scenario here (we come in with several potential death dates) an important teacher here, a terrible loss there, and some nice reprieves and (earned) rewards along the way, including sandwiches and a nap. This keeps life interesting, just like a good book. Seriously, as much as many people like to think an eternal vacation would please them, most of us are not inherent beach bums. Could you drink and tan all day, *every* day? Even beach bums surf, and that comes with its own problem set (No waves today! Bummer! Big wave kills me! Whoops). People who continue to do work they love live longer and healthier lives.

The point is there is no exact thing as "the future." It simply does not exist. Our futures are being refined every time we make new choices. That is, *if* we make new choices. Stay in that abusive marriage and you've got some heavy potential futures. Face your fears, leave the abusive marriage, and you've got new vistas and rewards awaiting. When we "do the work," new doors open magically. Open sesame. Every choice we make has ramifications. Just like a computer game.

I "chose" to lose my parents at an early age and to travel this life solo sans mate or kids (fun!). There's nothing I've wanted more than to create my own family. It has not happened. I had a bum first marriage that lasted a few acrid years and left me feeling lonelier and more disappointed than ever. I defend this marriage. I wanted it, and, on a soul level, I needed it. I regret nothing. However, it left a bad taste in my mouth. Loneliness and abandonment have been my karmic crosses to bear. Oh, and depression. What's loneliness and abandonment without a little depression to round out the landscape?

Over the years I've managed to pick myself up by the bootstraps, seeking guidance both within (meditation, self-reliance, journaling) and without (exercise and personal growth workshops). I've made a steady spiral upwards. However, every now and then I want reassurance from the spirit world that I will find love someday. I have been assured from the most elevated divine sources that this will indeed happen. However, they just won't say when, damn them. They're not allowed.

My burning question remains, "When will I get married?" To someone good, that is. Having already married the other kind, that particular (bad) husband created a whole new set of problems that only divorce could resolve—phew! But lo, these many years later, I am still wondering when my ideal (I did not say perfect) partner will manifest. Hence the many sessions I've had with prognosticators over the centuries. My mystery man remains less of a mystery due to all the hints, clues, and signs (many from my own dreams, which I trust implicitly) I've collected. He also remains absent from my daily life. *When* this relationship will commence remains…a mystery. "Come on, GOD!" I rail. "Throw me a BONE!" (How's that for Freudian?)

"Nope," says, God. "You'll just have to wait this one out."

I have a few answers penciled in, but my marital crossword puzzle remains unfinished.

There's nothing better than a good psychic or mediumistic reading. You feel your reader understands you, and he/she echoes or reinforces things you dream of or hope for. They acknowledge and sympathize with the challenges you've had (better yet, they can identify them). Occasionally someone will surprise, disturb, or displease you. That's okay, too. I've been puzzled or irritated during a reading only to get excited months or years later when I figured out what was actually implied by the vision. Often the seer may not even comprehend what he saw. Sometimes he'll misinterpret the information. (Remember, it's his mind interpreting your life. Who the hell is he?). Readings are not an exact science. You have to allow some flexibility for interpretation over time. One of those "the way will become clear" things.

Often you have to live your life and experience the event before the premonition makes any sense. A friend of mine is a devout, practically evangelical atheist. Years ago, she (a white girl) was on a date with an Asian fellow. After dinner they got psychic readings with someone at the restaurant, "for fun." My friend rolled her eyes when the psychic predicted, "You'll end up with someone foreign," since by the looks of her date (they were clearly together) she was already with him. However, perhaps twenty years later the memory of this message came back to haunt her. She had been with her life partner over ten years now. He's a white guy, but foreign, complete with accent. My friend, a New Yorker, lives in Europe with him. So that card reader accurately saw her future even though my friend thought it was a facile observation at the time.

A good reader takes dictation from her guides. She shares what the ethers provide: Visually (Clairvoyance), Aurally (Clairaudience), or through Feeling (Clairsentience). There are many ways to discern a message. And don't forget to pay attention to your dreams. This is where your own Higher Self, the Great Oz of Wisdom Within, and your Angels and Guides communicate with you. Sometimes they have to hit you over the head, even if you *are* willing to listen (and god forbid if you're not, imagine how much jumping up and down your guides have to do to get your attention). We're not always receptive (depends on how much TV we watch). Setting the intention to receive communication during your dreams and from your guides will greatly aid the process of your getting the information you want. And remember, you're not *supposed* to know everything. It would ruin the end of the movie.

A good channeled reading can also be life changing. Channeling is of a high spiritual order. Its intent is not to help you place bets at the track but to spiritually guide your journey. Soul stuff, not dating stuff. You don't listen to a good sermon or lecture to be told exactly what to do. You go to be inspired. It's up to you to figure out the specifics. That's 'cause it's your life. Wanting a quick fix or to be told what to do is passive and lazy. *The Sedona Journal of Emergence* is a monthly periodical of channeled inspirational readings that I swear by.

I have received amazing readings and stupid ones. Just because a reader has ability doesn't mean she's always right. Even painter Mary Cassatt threw out some of her sketches. Betty Friedan had to *work* that first draft of *The Feminine Mystique* before it was ready for publication. So without maligning the industry outright (I adore mystics), I will now share my critique of readings that were shameful, irresponsible, unprofessional, and just plain wrong.

No psychic is a crystal-clear crystal ball. Every orb has fingerprints on the surface or cracks within. The human psyche has many filters, that of personality, mood, and the vagaries of digestion (if the reader has had nothing for lunch vs. a pan of lasagna, I guarantee you'll get different readings). Can a good psychic read your probabilities and possibilities? Damn straight. What differentiates a good medium from a bad one is how these visions are *expressed*. Quick primer: A psychic knows/discerns things from the unseen. A medium hears/sees/talks to disembodied spirits. All mediums are psychic. Not all psychics are mediums. Got it? A medium has a communication skill set that goes beyond being psychic. They're like a human cell phone, picking up calls from disincarnates.

It's a clear rule of thumb never to give negative messages in a development circle (this is where psychics and mediums practice). These groups should be a safe place to practice, not to spew shadowy pronouncements, especially if you're not good at interpreting yet. When a symbol appears to the reader, she should ask first if it has meaning to the recipient. If it doesn't elicit an immediate response, the medium should shuffle through her mental Rolodex to see what associations come up, since Spirit is using the medium's mental vocabulary to filter its symbols through. If a message on the "heavy" side appears, there are ways to phrase it so that it does not come off as a frightening pronouncement. You certainly don't say, "You're going to die tomorrow." Even if they are. If in doubt about something dark, keep your mouth shut.

A young seer described a scary looking and "depressed" male skull for me. This image was neither fun, reassuring, nor helpful. She felt it was my father. An impossibility. My father was neither creepy nor depressed, though he was dead. That kind of a symbol for him was "dead" wrong. Then we guessed it was my uncle (I was grasping at straws as to who or what it could mean). However, my uncle was a happy go lucky guy, and while he had an amusing "shady" side, there was nothing creepy or depressed about him either. Souls at peace don't show up as skulls. That's for scary movies, not my living room. And that's where this reading took place. It couldn't be either of my grandfathers as they were loving, happy men. Quite simply, this depressed male "skull" was not mine.

Someone recently confirmed for me what I already knew. If a reader is getting dark images, it says something about the reader. Always? No. But if you're laying dark, creepy shit on my dad and uncle then you're way off course. And this reader wouldn't let up with it either. She was a member of the psychic development group I run, something that has evolved over time into a *spiritual* development group, with a smattering of psychic focus at the end, when all the meditating and praying has raised our spiritual energies considerably. To proceed with visionary work at this time inevitably produces clearer, more insightful messages because we are connected to the higher realms (vs. the lower astral, where darker energies lurk, a sort of morally smoggy zone). The messages coming from a spiritually uplifted plane are loving, educational, and directional. When the messages are dark or negative, I have a little talk with the reader.

"You're going to break your ankle," someone told me, seemingly with glee.

"Excuse me?"

"You're going to break your ankle but it's going to be okay because you're gonna meet this guy at the same time so it won't matter. But you'll be more focused on your ankle than on him, and he'll think it's funny."

As much as the "great guy" is a "great thing," this reader was inflicting bodily harm on me in the mental realm. She was also a member of my circle and I let her know that that was not a responsible message as she was planting the seed that I was going to break my ankle. She backpedaled by saying maybe I would just sprain it, maybe I wouldn't even hurt it, the point was the guy.

But that's not how she said it the first time, in front of a group. "You are going to break your ankle," were the words out of her mouth.

When someone is reading they have the power of authority. We tend to give our power away when we think someone has something we don't, like a psychic ability. Even psychics do this when someone else is reading them. Somebody may know or see something that you don't, particularly concerning your own life (since psychics can't particularly predict their own futures, including marriage partners, just ask Sylvia Browne about her numerous husbands). Actually, Sylvia Browne's book *Psychic* is not only damn good but really funny. Other psychics whose books and work I admire are Lisa Williams, James Van Praagh, and Colette Baron-Reid.

I told the "broken ankle" reader that a better way to phrase her original message would be, "There's a possibility you might hurt your ankle, so be careful. There may be a guy around, like a date, so it might involve high heels. You'll be having fun, don't worry, just be careful!" Then at least I'm not stuck with doom. I've already had serious injuries involving my ankle, my knee, and now my foot. Do I want more? No! Am I being careful with myself? Yes.

It's standard practice (among responsible readers) not to give negative messages. Why? Because they predispose people toward that dark potentiality. Beware of any reader or gypsy who intones ominously about your life. We all have negative stuff and people in our life to some extent. There's nothing wrong in identifying it and suggesting a course of action. But beware of people whose intent is to *scare* you. That makes you vulnerable, and often this type of manipulator (this is a classic ploy) tells you that you need their help to remove the curse or to give you insight or...*RUN*, don't walk away from this nonsense. Do you feel better or worse after the reading? Trust your feelings.

Somerset Maugham illustrates the power of suggestion in his short story, "Appointment in Samarra." A master sends his servant to do an errand in Baghdad, where the servant startles to see Death staring at him. The servant trembles, runs, then flees to Samarra to hide. While in Samarra he bumps right into Death. Death slaps his knee and says, "What a hoot to see you in Baghdad! Our appointment wasn't until here, today...You're right on time."

Wink, wink! You can't escape your destiny (if it's one of your big plot points). If you saw the movie *Fargo*, you may remember the scene where the kidnapped wife is so petrified of her captors (that she has temporarily escaped) that she runs screaming in terror out from behind the shower curtain, where she was hiding, right into their arms. It was hysterically funny because it was psychologically true. We do ourselves in with our fears, often making them self-fulfilling prophecies.

Sometimes psychic "pros" have said things that, while not negative, still bothered or depressed me because they were not what I wanted to hear. An example. I was involved in an ucky dating situation involving the aforementioned short, curly haired guy with glasses. I wanted to know more but there was no more to know, since he and I were going nowhere, to my dismay. The cards revealed that the relationship was on hold (he was away, it turns out, at some depraved Sandals-type resort for perverts). My friend looked at her cards and made the most hysterical assortment of hemming and hawing sounds. Without uttering a word, she formed her conclusion by shaking her head then said, "There's someone else. Pull three more cards." I didn't want to hear about anyone else. I wanted to hear about the elusive pervert. I was dissatisfied by her reading because she didn't say what I wanted to hear. But what she said was true.

The next three cards indicated a cop, a lawyer, or military guy, all ridiculous suggestions for me. She said, "He's an authority," (King of Swords). And finally, "It's destiny," (the Star card). Four months later I met this man, a famous authority I had admired from afar. Difficult as this relationship was, it was destiny, for sure. We kicked the karma out of each other.

I came away from that dark destiny and walked right into the arms of another dark and depressing fellow (who, of course, I thought was sweet and delightful when I met him). I was in such a bleak space there was no way I could attract (or more to the point, be attracted to) a happy, upbeat guy. Law of Attraction. I was in the dumps. I got dumpy guys.

Well, Diane, a dear spiritual friend of mine often gave me psychic readings on my birthday since she knew that my burning question, "Where is my mate?" continued to smolder.

Diane paid for a phone reading for me with someone who had given her a good phone reading. I wanted to focus on relationships. She said there were three guys in my energy field and that they were present or future, not past. One, it turned out, was a dull acquaintance who was not on my romantic radar in any way, shape, or form. So who cared if he liked me? Next, she got all excited. She described this nice, attractive, successful, athletic fellow with whom I could have fun. FUN, you say? Happy, successful, healthy? I was irritated, being currently in love (or rather, obsessed) with a bleak, dark, but very bright and talented musician (the guy I thought was sweet and delightful for the first ten minutes). I asked her to focus on this Darth Vader (I'm guessing he was the third guy in my energy field after 1) Boring Guy and 2) Good Guy).

She nailed him. "He's the type that sees the sediment in the glass."

Yes, he was a "glass-half-empty" type, as glum and plodding as Eeyore. Of *course*, I loved him. Oy.

I enjoyed a full three years of emotional torture with this fellow. He never indulged me with sex, damn him, and perhaps, when all is said and done, it was for the best. It remained a torturous relationship nonetheless. A bit of cat and mouse, a bit of emotional S&M, a bit of fuck me/fuck you, without any actual fucking going on. Sigh...

At any rate, as I got healthier and happier (Thank god, actually, thank Me, I'm the one that made it happen) "creepy-let me-down-guy" was losing his appeal, and I was establishing boundaries that made it easier to keep him out. Lesson learned: you don't date *talent*. I don't care how famous, smart, or skilled someone is, at the end of the day, it is the PERSON you're dating, not their skill set. How does the PERSON treat you? Is your "medal" sporting soldier a miserable Great Santini? Dr. Phil once said something that struck me hard. A woman was pining for her ex (he was not pining for her) who treated her terribly.

Dr. Phil said, "Do you miss *him*, or the fantasy of who you wish he was?"

Bingo! Half of us are living in our minds and ignoring the reality punching us in the face.

I was thrilled to be able to finally quote the founder of Rational Emotive Behavior Therapy to the mean musician—after he stood me up then *yelled at me*—I wrote him, "The fact that your father beat you and your mother was an alcoholic is not the reason you are an asshole today." – Albert Ellis

Yes! He had excuses for everything, but the bottom line was he was a rude, lying, son of a bitch. His "problems" included being a successful musician, if you can believe that (and he did). Nothing excused his excruciatingly cold and cruel behavior.

Anyway, now that I'm happier, (praise Me and Jesus), *I can't wait for the nice guy to get here*. But the point of my going down this expository detour is because, when the phone reading was over with this psychic, I wasn't in a particularly good mood. She said plenty of stuff I *didn't* want to hear, including that *there was some nice, handsome, successful guy who would be a great match for me*. The nerve of her. Since I was entranced with the dark side this was not news I wanted. Now, I think it's fantastic. No psychic will tell me when it will start. How much happier do I have to get, dammit?

Conversely, and surprisingly, you have to know when *not* to tell good news. My psychic cousin Genia's grandmother was also psychic. Grandma Sappho (now in spirit) gave a reading to a married woman who was dying to get pregnant. Sappho didn't see a thing. Nada. No babies. She sent the barren woman packing. When she left, Sappho told family that this woman would get pregnant within three months (which she did). Had she told the girl that, she felt it would have interfered with her destiny. Sappho was a responsible reader. Not everything should be known. Some things must be lived (like my interminable singlehood).

Back to examples of "sketchy" readings. I wrote to a medical intuitive whose column I read. When I asked her what I could do to improve my health, she told me I needed to eat more whole grains, fiber, and fruit then proceeded to list exactly what I just had for lunch. She wasn't *prescribing*, she was *describing*. The only suggestion I took was to add vitamin C to my diet. Since I already ate fruit I bought supplements—you can't OD on C. Some believe super doses are super healthy and my body feels good with the added dose. So score one for my intuition, because that's ultimately what I listened to in deciding to take her advice. Remember, it's always up to you what you do or don't do. If you follow someone's advice, you are choosing to do so. Don't blame them if it doesn't work out. Take responsibility for your actions. No one *makes* you do anything.

Then I asked another psychic about the *timing* of my next relationship. My question was WHEN? That was it. I asked, "Do you have any idea about the timing of this relationship?" She proceeded to make sweeping generalizations about all men and all of my interactions with them. "You need to be careful of men. They will be angry and you will be to blame."

Excuse me?

She accurately generalized that my past 20 years have not been easy for relationships (I had the marriage and a few intense, but short-lived relationships). None of them were ideal partnerships. All of them were riveting, melodramatic, and exactly what I wanted at the time: terrific learning experiences fraught with anxiety and drama, which made them "interesting" (if not relaxing).

She suggested that I should marry a man that travels a lot or that I should travel a lot because I "love my space" and I can't have him underfoot for long. "It would destroy the marriage."

I found the whole reading offensive and it is my Exhibit A for "How to Give a Bad Psychic Reading." I'm not even with this guy yet, and she's already telling me to play it loose? Too much togetherness will *destroy* the marriage?

The last guy I dated was older and very set in his ways. He suggested we live in separate homes (he used Tim Burton and Helena Bonham Carter as the model). Thanks, but that's not my idea of how a couple functions. In fact, when I got married, I changed my name to his because I felt that's what families did. You were one unit, and I wanted to have kids. After the divorce I changed my name back right quick and I will not change my name again when I get re-married. A marriage is not based on names. But I draw the line at "his and her" homes.

What she diagnosed as my "problem" could have been phrased like this so it's not totally obnoxious: "Because you are an independent Aquarius, make sure you and your partner figure out how to enjoy each other's company but also have your own space." Do you see how that is expressing the same sentiment, without predicting doom, divorce, and implying I can't be with someone for too long? (which sure sounds like a character flaw to me).

I quote her again because this just blew my mind: "You need to be careful of men because they can have an anger problem and which will lead to a divorce. You usually have very intense relationships and you never know where you stand."

I need to be careful of men? All men? I don't know all men. Every man I know is different from every other man I know (except the ones I've dated—they were all alike). The better way to phrase this would be: "You need to avoid *men with anger problems*. It is possible that you often didn't know where you stood with the men you've been with."

Don't state anything definitively. This is a subjective business. It's about tendencies, possibilities, and probabilities, not about facts.

She generalized again. "It is *always* very exciting at the beginning and *it ends up* as you being the bad guy. *They will put the blame on you and you will believe it.*" (The bad English is hers, not mine).

Nothing is always anything, honey bunny. Even my progression of angry narcissists had a nice trajectory, each one getting better than the last in some small but creepy way. Second, none of my relationships were exciting in the beginning. They all started casually, and while I got excited as the intrigue developed, there was never a honeymoon period, if you will. So if you want to call my being strung out and anxious as "exciting," go to, oh great seer.

I was excited, but not because it was healthy or mutual in any way. Nor was I the bad guy. While I'm sure my partners had plenty to whine about (they whined about everything, so why not about me?) my problem was being overly understanding and compassionate to fellows who didn't appreciate it (a mistake I'll not make again). In fact, many of 'em came crawling back in one form or another, which always surprised me, given how apathetic they were at the time we dated. Apparently, I give good memory. I most certainly have cast my pearls before swine. Soo-ee!

She went on: "I know you want to know more about the man. I feel he wears a brown or possible blue uniform with a label on the pocket of where he works. He is a mechanic of some kind and very much a family man. I feel that you will meet him but it necessary doesn't mean he is the right man. (*What the fuck does that mean?*). Just wait and go slow in a relationship. (*Exactly what a person who ONLY wants to know WHEN wants to hear*). The signs will be there. (*What signs? That's why I reached out to YOU!*).

Brown uniform could be UPS. And a mechanic? I don't even have a car. I have nothing against blue-collar guys, but they are not my type. They are my cousin's type. She married a mechanic (Joey Buttafuoco's moral equivalent). I am not maligning all mechanics, just Joey Buttafuoco and my cousin's ex, a primo deadbeat dad. Why did my cousin, a psychic, marry this buffoon? One, she loved him. Two, psychics can't see their own future. Three, he was her karma. Psychics have to learn from their choices the way the rest of us putzes do.

I can verify/adapt the following from what this psychic wrote me: I have had relationships with angry men. I was off guard, never knew where I stood (actually, I did—it was usually in the dog house). They took their anger out on me. It was exciting in the beginning if you call my wondering if/when they would call and if/when I would ever see them again exciting. I am very independent and love my space, but I expect to be with a self-contained man who is peaceful, so that we can cohabit peacefully. I've been single most of my life. I want to be with the love of my life when I'm finally with him, not book vacations at separate time-shares. The bottom line is that I asked this woman *one* question and one question only. Did she have any sense of *when* my next serious relationship would begin? That is the only thing she had no comment on. So thanks for the bang-up bad reading!

Here's another sure sign of a bad reading. A medium who came highly recommended kept pulling names out of the air, none of which I could identify as dead friends or relatives. The only names she didn't try on me were Larry, Curly, and Moe. Occasionally, she would start to describe someone that I might know, but then she'd blow it. For instance, while describing a person I could identify, say Snow White, she'd blurt out, "She has dark hair and pale skin..." I was starting to get the picture, yes! "She weighs 400 pounds..." No, I didn't know her. She mixed metaphors and dead people. Her (bad) reading was utterly useless to me.

My diagnosis? She was not disciplined. I don't doubt that she has ability, however, if you don't know how to tame it, you're like a bucking bronco. When you're psychically open you get lots of information, some of which is psychic static, white noise from the ethers. Just like a research scientist or a detective, you have to learn what to weed out. Mediums go to school to hone their skills, including the highly respected Arthur Findley College in England.

I will add to this that the best mediums I've known were mentally sharp and/or well educated enough to understand the references and information coming through them. The spirit world uses your mental abilities and vocabulary to filter their messages. The more you know, the easier they can express themselves.

Here's an example of a reading years ago that wasn't bad, but it only skirted the edges of what I wanted to know. The psychic said, "There is a mate for you, younger, dark, curly hair, short with glasses." This depressed me because it was contradictory to what a channeled spirit (that I highly respected) told me, that my life's partner was older and taller than me, among a few other vaguely specific descriptors. The channel couldn't give me too much information about Mr. Right or I'd miss all the Mr. Goodbars I was destined to date. Years later I realized this psychic was right. He very clearly described someone physically (he neglected to mention all the neuroses) in my future, but who in no way, shape or form was my mate. He was anecdotal material, not marital material, someone to write about, not write *home* about. It wasn't love, it was just a passing fanny (you get the picture). Just because psychics see things doesn't mean they know what they are.

One psychic gave me very good advice. She was as fluttery as a butterfly and a hummingbird combined. Her very hyper energy made it hard to keep up with her insights. I told her about a dream I had years ago about my future mate, and while I couldn't see his face he *was* wearing a nametag. I was convinced that I now knew my mate's first and last name. How weird was that? Knowing a guy's name before even meeting him? Well, month after month and year after year went by without my meeting *anyone* with either the first or last name. I grew to hate that name and the unfulfilled dreams it implied. So I asked this psychic what she thought about it.

She said sagely, "Hold on to the name. It's not necessarily his name, but it could be tied to him in some way. For instance, you could be having dinner with him on a first date when you overhear someone say the name. It could be a business associate of his. It will be a *marker* to you that you're on the right track." She gave a very clear example of how this works. A client of hers was looking to buy a new home. She said, "You will know your house when you walk up slate steps to the front door and a leaf will blow across your foot." While they were wrapping up the session the customer's husband called to say he just found a new house on the market in the neighborhood where they were looking. Everyone got excited. Wife met husband at the house. Lo and behold, there were slate steps leading to the front door. Goosebumps. As she approached the steps with anticipation, a gust of autumnal wind blew a leaf over her foot. Amazing! She and her husband went inside. They looked around. Is this our new home? While in the kitchen, she looked out the window and from *that* vantage point saw *a home across the street that they ended up buying.* So the slate, the wind, the leaves, and the house itself were markers, like Hansel and Gretel's trail of breadcrumbs.

I've been told my mate is an ironworker named Jeffrey, the UPS guy, and a mechanic.

I know different. While it's fun to collect potential data from other psychics and friends, like picking flowers from a field, it's my own intuition, gut feelings, and dreams I rely on to create my bouquet. Use your intuition, common sense, and gut feelings in selecting a reader. Say a little prayer, requesting a "most benevolent outcome" (this is Tom T. Moore's prayer) that the ideal reader be brought to you with messages and insight that will be accurate and useful, and that the results will be better than you could hope or expect. Whether people are psychic sourpusses or secular ones, don't keep negative voices in your life, your heart, or your mind. If you are a reader, intend or pray that the highest information comes through you and will be of greatest good to your client. Be judicious with your words. We must all be wise. We must all be kind.

CHAPTER 5

The Big Black Box

My mother had terrible eyesight. A tomboy as a kid (she was a lanky, female version of Spanky from "Our Gang"), she grew into a slender and athletic beauty. Of Greek origin, her parents were from Chios (Mom) and Patras (Dad). Mom was born in Springfield, Mass, and moved to New York City in 1926, when she was six. She, her brother Pete, and her parents Iphigenia and Christos lived in the building directly next to the one I live in now, her street address just three digits away from that of my current apartment. My mother lived in my current home, too, so she spent most of her life in the same neighborhood on the same street. So have I.

I recently learned that my folks even met at a YWCA in this neighborhood. I knew they met at a Y mixer after the war, but I didn't find out until this month that it was the very Y where I took tap class, played ping-pong with my mother, and swam in the pool as a kid. This neighborhood has my family written all over it.

Much to her dismay, my mother needed glasses. Also to her dismay, she had short, straight eyelashes. While in grade school she curled them up into the crease of her eye to effect a "curl" during class. I can't imagine it worked but it was important for her to try. Despite the short straight lashes, the glasses (which she took off every chance she got), and what she considered to be an overlarge nose (I begged to differ with her), she was a glamorous gal, a 1930s and '40s "doll" right out of the popular Frank Loesser musical.

TV never took center stage in our home, although my folks got one in the 1950s along with the rest of America. When I was a tot I came back very excited from school one day and told Mom about a brand new Muppet show for kids premiering that afternoon. She said, "Sesame seeds? That's funny...I just bought some at the health food store." I watched *Star Trek* and *The Twilight Zone* with my sister in the '60s, and *All in the Family*, *Rhoda*, *Maude*, *Sanford and Son*, *The Jeffersons*, and *Good Times* with my mom in the '70s.

My folks had a big clunky set like everyone else in the 1950s. But the TV I remember most is the last one my mother owned, a white plastic 17-inch Panasonic black and white number from the 1970s, complete with rabbit-ears antennae. Mom kept it in her bedroom on a TV table, the kind most people put food on. By this time she had been widowed (and single) for many years. She put curlers in her short brown hair (she gave up on the lashes decades ago) and lay in bed in her rather glamorous carnelian-red robe with gold-brocade ribbon camouflaging its lengthwise zipper. The final touch to her signature look was bottle-thick, cat glasses right out of a Gary Larson cartoon. She was nearsighted, legally blind, and never drove a car.

Her black and white TV was *Jetsons* cool. It could have been from the set of *2001: A Space Odyssey*, or Woody Allen's *Sleeper*. The unit sported rounded-square white plastic design, something Apple might have claimed if they were making TVs. In fact, the Lifesaver colored iMac units (I had one in "grape") were highly reminiscent of this mod, plastic TV. Cute though it was, it got fairly dirty with static, the picture was black and white, and at 17 inches, it was the antithesis of today's giant flat screens. Mom kept it six feet away from her bed, the requisite distance so evil TV radiation didn't affect her, or me. Mom was concerned with "rays," pesticides, drugs, and doctors. She took me to chiropractors and homeopaths and gave me vitamins, never drugs. I was not inoculated. She peeled apples for my school lunch so I wouldn't eat the skin (which holds the highest percentage of pesticides). I would have preferred a Yodel or Ring Ding like normal kids, but now I understand. She was trying to keep me away from the Kryptonite, both the visible and the invisible kinds. I now do the same for myself and my pets.

My sister convinced my mom to get a big color TV, one she could see without squinting or having to guess what was on the screen. We went down to J&R Music World on Park Row in lower Manhattan (I just wrote "Park Place" erroneously. That would exist in lower "Monopoly"). I was terribly excited. This was the big time for Mom and me. Mom was hesitant, but allowed my sister to drive us downtown to pick up Black Beauty. Mom was cautious with expenditures and indulgences. But since her life was restrictive, particularly the last few years when she was gravely ill, the color TV seemed a wise choice.

We unpacked the unit and, breathless, turned it on to—static. Mom could get a "decent" picture (if you had her very low, black and white standards) with her Panasonic and its rabbit-ears antennae. This baby produced *nothing* but loud, colorful interference. Without cable it would not perform, and my mother would not add insult to injury by paying more (for cable) after paying more for a new TV. Back it went to the store. With her crappy eyesight what the hell difference did it make how clear the picture was anyway?

My mother did allow herself one indulgence before dying. She got cataract surgery the last summer of her life. It was as if she'd won the lottery. She repeated, "I can see! I can see!!!" over and over, in wonder and ecstasy each and every day like a kid on Christmas, even though she was dying of cancer. Had she opted for that surgery a week before she died I would have said, "Go for it, Mom," for the pleasure it gave her. She got larger, roundish, more au courant frames with light-as-air lenses, and joyously tossed out the coke bottle contraption that had been the bane of her existence. Hers was a thrilling new lease on life, a "free at last, free at last, thank God Almighty, I'm free at last!" reprieve. Her imminent physical release and rebirth into Spirit must have felt just like that, too.

Following my mother's death in 1985, I made one of my first major purchases, a color TV. A Sony Trinitron, I bought the floor model at Crazy Eddie's for $400 and change. I still have it. It still works. But over the years as I've become increasingly spiritual and New Age I've read warnings from numerous teachers (mostly disembodied, via channeled readings and books) that TV was not just the "Idiot Box" (as my father called it) but a vehicle of the dark forces controlling the population (watch the movie *THRIVE* online for free, and check out *Zeitgeist* as well). This may sound way out there to some of you, but mind control is not a new concept. It's real and palpable. Advertising is mind control. We are being influenced all the time and scientific studies prove it. After watching (or just hearing) a couple of commercials are you hungry? Of course, you are. After eating some crap food when you weren't even hungry, are you fatter? Of course, you are! Since you're fat and inactive from watching so much TV now you need other products the TV and magazines (any mass media) sells: diet aids, diet soda, diets, antiperspirants, and anti-depressants. Oh, and don't forget a new car, bigger home, and bigger boobs, all available at your local mall.

The more you watch, the more you need. Paddy Chayefsky's opus, *Network* covered this terrain to great, good effect without invoking the spirit world. TV may turn its viewers into pawns, but it's not manned by idiots by a long shot. There have been sinister forces at work keeping the public-at-large fat, passive, mesmerized, and shopping.

In a script note Chayefsky described TV as "an indestructible and terrifying giant that is stronger than the government." In another note, "We are not dealing with a human institution. We are dealing with an enormous profit-making machine." By the end of his script he concluded with yet another note, "*All the networks will have been bought by other multinationals.*" Multinationals. Corporations. The Military Industrial Complex. The Corporatocracy. They are one. The government has been doing their bidding, not ours—the people by and for whom this country was fought and founded. President Eisenhower warned of this takeover in his televised farewell speech. Indulge me as I continue to explore with you.

"In Zombie Land you stare at TV in a trance, your brain filled with images of news & stories that are not real. It is virtual reality. Real life is going on in your living room, but your mind is elsewhere. TV reduces intelligence & destroys the immune system. Nothing can control you if you activate and utilize your power & stop feeling like a victim. ALL of your responses to human suffering are being utilized as a method to manipulate your feelings. You are being impulsed to feel afraid, angry, sad, helpless, bruised, desperate and raw. The more you respond to things across the world you have no part of, the more you ignore things that need to be taken care of right in front of your noses. It's intentional distraction. These dramas are set up to distract you from seeing The Beautiful New Reality that is building and getting ready to split off from Zombie Land. Forget TELL-A-VISION. Get your OWN VISION" (Barbara Hand Clow, *The Pleiadian Agenda*). The alpha brain waves induced by watching TV pave the way for the brainwashing that TV produces.

"In November 1969, a researcher named Herbert Krugman, who later became manager of public-opinion research at General Electric headquarters in Connecticut, decided to try to discover what goes on physiologically in the brain of a person watching TV. He elicited the co-operation of a twenty-two-year-old secretary and taped a single electrode to the back of her head. The wire from this electrode connected to a Grass Model 7 Polygraph, which in turn interfaced with a Honeywell 7600 computer and a CAT 400B computer.

"Flicking on the TV, Krugman began monitoring the brain-waves of the subject. What he found through repeated trials was that within about thirty seconds, the brain-waves switched from predominantly beta waves, indicating alert and conscious attention, to predominantly alpha waves, indicating an unfocused, receptive lack of attention: the state of aimless fantasy and daydreaming below the threshold of consciousness. When Krugman's subject turned to reading through a magazine, beta waves reappeared, indicating that conscious and alert attentiveness had replaced the daydreaming state."

"What surprised Krugman, who had set out to test some (Marshall) McLuhan-esque hypotheses about the nature of TV-viewing, was how rapidly the alpha-state emerged. Further research revealed that the brain's left hemisphere, which processes information logically and analytically, tunes out while the person is watching TV. This tuning-out allows the right hemisphere of the brain, which processes information emotionally and non-critically, to function unimpeded. 'It appears,' wrote Krugman in a report of his findings, 'that the mode of response to television is more or less constant and very different from the response to print. That is, the basic electrical response of the brain is clearly to the medium and not to content difference.... (Television is) a communication medium that effortlessly transmits huge quantities of information not thought about at the time of exposure.'" (Joyce Nelson, *The Perfect Machine*.)

I took a college class on the media in the early '80s. It was considered "a gut" and attracted many a football player. I, on the other hand, as an actress, was genuinely interested in the material. My professor was a short, slightly round, white-haired man who had been a part owner of a Boston TV station. He clued us in to some of the simplistic generalizations of 1970's TV-writing, such as how criminals were usually represented as white, how all rich people were bad, all poor people were good, even though these scripts were being written by very rich white people. The man wasn't racist. He was pointing out inconsistencies and hypocrisies within the biz. He figured some of it came from guilt and liberal inclinations. He shared a statistic that most of the poor people in this country were white and that most of us aren't racist, but classist. His example was if you were alone at night you might be wary if you saw a thuggish white male wearing, oh, say, a hoodie, but would probably not be worried if you eyed a professional black male in a 3-piece suit in your vicinity. It was the socio-economic class that was of greater concern, not race. He was asking us to think "outside of the box" as it were. The nickname for this class was "TV."

Our one homework assignment was to follow a weekly, one-hour TV show (hence the popularity of this class). I chose Ripley's *Believe It Or Not* hosted by creepy Jack Palance. My college roommate ended up with him in a hotel elevator somewhere. Jack bemoaned to his companion the amount of time it took for the elevator to elevate him. When he arrived at his floor, Kathleen piped up, "You made it! Believe it, or not!"

My professor told us, "In the future news will become sensational. The line will blur between news and entertainment." How could that be? Walter Cronkite *entertaining*? The whole point of news was to be boring and black & white like newsprint, wasn't it? I thought his projection was strange but I liked the guy. He was amiable and insightful. (The films *Broadcast News* and *Wag the Dog* explored early on what my professor said and what is now observable fact).

Prof gave us a comprehensive, "suggested" reading list. They were fascinating books, all of which I read and none of whose titles I can remember. The only thing that was required was the one hour of TV viewing. The football players, being academic minimalists, chose not to take his suggestions. They devoted themselves to the hour of mandatory TV. Teach made a point of announcing grades as he handed back our midterm tests. The football team fumbled at the fourth down, getting D's and F's. I scored a touchdown.

I mention this professor because one of the facts he shared with us was that when you are watching the scariest movie on TV, sweating bullets, on the edge of your seat, hyperventilating, and with heart pounding, you are still engaging/creating fewer brain waves than if you were reading the dictionary (echoing author Joyce Nelson's book excerpt, above). As much as I love words, the dictionary is a snooze-fest as far as entertainment goes. Reading engages the brain. Watching TV does not. The real *Zombieland* is not on the screen. It is on our couches.

Now that I've explored the academic, literary, and scientific grievances regarding the idiot box, on to the weirdo New Age warnings. Even when your TV/Cable box is off, it emits inaudible vibrations, waves, or tones that are detrimental and demoralizing to the human. Obviously, this is not provable. Besides, we barely question the effects of the known invisible rays we are constantly subjecting ourselves to. We're too obsessed with our toys to contemplate getting rid of them, even to avoid brain tumors. And who ever got a brain tumor from their cell phone? On the other hand, cancer rates are higher than ever. Microwaves, x-rays, cell phones, computers, TV and radio waves, airport security, MRIs, mammograms, and electric appliances produce endless sources of exposure in our techno-crazy age. While I was open to the nefarious "damned if it's on, damned if it's off" TV theory (you could also say they're dumbing us down simply by airing Snooki and Fox TV), that didn't mean I was actually going to get rid of my TV. TV is many a person's security blanket and default best friend. It's the blow-up sex-doll of the entertainment world.

The spirits and guides proceeded to pronounce microwaves' malevolence. The waves they zap the food with kill the subtle "prana" of your food (assuming it had any to begin with since most people eat over-processed calories devoid of any actual nutrition). Rent *Food Matters, Hungry for Change, Crazy, Sexy Cancer, The Beautiful Truth, Supersize Me, Fat, Sick and Nearly Dead,* and

The Corporation. We need greens in our diet, nature in our lives, and truth and peace instead of dissonance and distraction.

Our goal need not be "perfection," but we don't have to submit to obesity, depression, consumerist frenzy, debt, and prescription-pill addiction. Guess who benefits from all that? The Corporations. We've been subjected to a very successful addiction experiment by Madison Avenue and the Corporations that fund it (and who own the food and drug companies). We've been their fat, sick, poor, and nearly dead human guinea pigs and pawns for quite some time now. Our obesity, depression, diabetes, high cholesterol, high blood pressure, cancer, and heart disease rates attest to it.

What's the radical solution? Turn off the TV! Throw out your microwave! Read a book! Call a friend. Better yet, *meet* with a friend. Remember "real" face time, like with a face, not an iPhone? Ride your bike. *Get* a bike. Cook some fresh food. Grow a garden. Make soup. Find a hobby. Join a group. *Start* a group. Meditate. Pray. Dance. Scream. Swim. Jump up and down. Hoot and holler. Adopt a dog. Adopt a cat. Blow bubbles. Chew gum. Get a social life. Jump rope. Take a *nap*. Help someone. Help yourself.

Humans are social animals, and we've been reduced to solitary confinement in our own living rooms. How did we allow this to happen? Yes, we've willingly participated in "their" evil experiment, lulled by our fancy toys, delusions, and illusions, just like Pinocchio on Pleasure Island and humans in *The Matrix* (which perfectly dramatizes our abuse by cold, dark forces). We've been manipulated and brainwashed. You don't have to get mad as hell. But you do have to do something about it. Action is required; to activate brain waves, a human life, and a planet. Just like little Milo in *The Phantom Tollbooth*, when he stops paying attention and ends up stuck in The Doldrums, the only way he can get out of his virtual quicksand is to start thinking. And fast.

I was unnerved when I learned of the "evil rays" coming through my TV, playing with my mind and my moods. Author/lecturer David Icke, Alex Jones, and Jesse Ventura spearhead conspiracy theory warpaths. (Some of it is way out there, but truth is often stranger than fiction). When I told a successful screenwriter friend of mine about the TV-microwave-dark-forces manipulating humans theory, he said, "There's a movie about just that called *They Live*." I rented it immediately.

"*They Live* is a 1988 science fiction/horror film directed by John Carpenter, who also wrote the screenplay under the pseudonym Frank Armitage. Part science fiction, part dark comedy, the film echoes contemporary fears of a declining economy, within a culture of greed and conspicuous consumption common among Americans. In *They Live*, the ruling-class within the moneyed elite is, in fact, aliens managing human social affairs through the use of a signal on top of the TV broadcast that is concealing their appearance and subliminal messages in mass media." (Wikipedia).

There are many channeled books on the topic, including *Bringers of the Dawn*, by Barbara Marciniak, *No More Secrets, No More Lies*, by Patricia Cori, and *The Pleiadian Agenda*, by Barbara Hand Clow.

But was I actually going to throw my TV out? Alien manipulation or not, I was single, heck, I was American, no, I was HUMAN, and TV is an intrinsic part of most of our lives. You'd no sooner think of getting rid of your set than you would your refrigerator or car, right? When I counseled a friend who was having considerable money problems, made worse by a sky-high cable bill, I told him to get rid of cable. Without a beat he replied, "I'd rather not eat."

I consoled myself by saying, "well, I only watch the GOOD stuff (ha ha), you know, PBS, *Judge Judy*, forensics shows, Bill Maher, *The Sopranos*, and HBO comedy specials."

There was no way I was getting rid of my TV, aliens or no. Until the day they doubled my cable bill. I had just lost my job and health insurance and had severely fucked up my knee in a bike accident. I sat alone in my hot apartment without lights or air conditioning for fear of running up the electric bill. I was in suspended animation fueled by fear and despair, a decidedly un-fun, unproductive mode.

Desperate to turn things around I prayed for help with my financial and career woes one night and the very next day a book title popped into my head over breakfast, *The Wealthy Spirit* by Chellie Campbell. I was overjoyed that Spirit answered so quickly and perfectly. I thanked my Guides and Guardians. This is a smart, fun and helpful book about how to create abundance in your life by happy means and smart business decisions. It had been sitting unread on my bookshelf for months and is one in a long line of inspired books, movies, friends, seminars, and experiences that have led me to the amazing place I am in just four short years later. I've passionately cleaved to my heart's desires while simultaneously exorcising people, jobs, and circumstances that were anathema to me. I followed the Yellow Brick road and now live in Emerald City, free from corporate indentured servitude (I used to work for AIG and other hellish corporate black ops).

At any rate, my cable bill automatically went on my credit card so I didn't notice initially that it had doubled for the past several months from a reasonable fee to a decidedly unreasonable one. I flipped out and called the cable company. They hadn't even warned me about the increase. They just slipped it in. The young lady on the other end was very nice, but she couldn't adjust the past two months' financial wreckage. She offered to lower my bill to keep me as a customer. When her lowest offer was still higher than what I'd originally paid I made a life changing decision. "Shut it off," I blurted.

"What?" she responded, her mental operating system utterly confounded by my request.

You'd think I'd asked her to shoot me in the head. She became a malfunctioning droid from *Westworld* or *The Stepford Wives*.

"Request does not compute. Repeat. Request does not compute," her silence screamed.

I rephrased my statement so she could absorb it fully. "Take it away. I can't afford it. I don't want it. Kaput. Niente. Finito. Sayonara." There was continued silence on the other end. Plenty of people get their cable turned off because they didn't pay the bill, but how many do you know who got rid of cable "just because?" In a blaze of glory I proclaimed my freedom from the Aliens and Time Warner Cable (and/or the Aliens of Time Warner Cable).

Central Computer turned off my "life support" within minutes. I returned my dead cable box to Central Computer the next day and returned to a silent home. Silent, hot, and painful, since my knee was still the size of a cantaloupe. I went cold turkey. When I told my senior neighbor Shirley what happened she readied to call an ambulance. Not for my knee. For my dementia.

"*What do you mean you don't have TV????!!!!*"

I was thrilled because I was finally listening to my disembodied spiritual gurus who said, "Seriously, *get rid of your TV.*"

So I did it for financial reasons versus giving it up for lent, but nonetheless the deed was done. I still have the Sony Trinitron. I used it with my DVD player, but even that broke down a month or two ago, which meant I couldn't watch Netflix rentals on a big screen. I decided to buy a small, cheap DVD player that claimed compatibility with older TV sets. Apparently, 1985 is older than "old." It is antediluvian. I repacked the tiny black box and decided to go even colder turkey; I would get rid of the Big Black Box itself, releasing my 1985 Sony Trinitron to the good people of Goodwill. I'm left with my 13-inch MAC laptop. I watch movies at a distance from my desk in a comfy chair. If there are subtitles, I'm screwed. Yes, a simple life, practically Amish, Quaker, Shaker, and Puritan by Manhattan standards.

Then it hit me, I'm right back where my mom was, and I've outdone her with an even smaller screen. Of course, it's color, not black and white, and my eyesight is perfect, but still, it's bare bones by today's "entertainment center" standards. Heck, it's bare bones compared to my 19-inch 4,000 pound Trinitron days of yore when I could actually read subtitles. Mom's TV was unceremoniously marched back to J&R Music World, and my dinky new DVD player was flung back to China by way of Target.

The Trinitron was relegated to the floor. Buddha, Ganesh, and candles, which adorned the top of my DVD player, then the top of my TV (when the DVD player died), will now adorn actual wood, not a plastic contraption filled with tubes and things that attract static dirt and emit evil rays whether on or off. The Trinitron unleashed one final act of virulent aggression against me as I prepared to throw it over the cliff. It wasn't going down without a fight. Since I could slide it easily on the sideboard to clean underneath, it's true heft remained concealed. As I hoisted it I realized what a true monster it was. If I let go, it would be totaled, a pile of crushed cathode ray tubes. If I pulled it back up, I'd just have to start all over again. I battled this monster down to the ground like Gandalf in blitzkrieg with the Balrog at the Bridge of Khazad-dûm. I prayed quickly to not die or at least not to get too hurt. The Balrog won. My back went out and I had to go to my chiropractor, twice. But I got it to the floor in one piece. My microwave had already been dismissed two years ago. Valerie Two, Radiation Monsters, Zero. It's a new day for me.

When I lived in the country for two months at a personal growth program, I watched no TV (there was none there to be watched) and I lost weight. I was in terrific shape. My exercise was comprised of working out my mind, heart, and emotions and taking easy afternoon walks down country roads. Being out of the city and in nature alone was healing.

"Trusting our messages and walking away from the computer in complete faith that all will be well has been a tremendous detachment effort on your part. This brings you closer to Oneness, whether you believe it or not. Your mind/logic made you THINK you were connected only by your Internet connection, but many of you are quickly discovering that you are closer to Oneness when you connect through your heart and feelings rather than mind/logic/seeing. Kudos to those of you who have taken this courageous step. For those of you who have not yet moved out of the shallow end without your flotation devices, it is time to learn to swim in deeper waters. Give it a try! We guarantee you will float just fine." Channeled by Jen Freer, "Freer Spirit" (freerspirit.com).

Is sitting in front of your computer all day and night any better than sitting in front of the boob tube? I'm not throwing out my computer, or my cell phone. But I leave the house, eat well, exercise, meditate, express myself creatively, have friends, a full spiritual life, and read books. We all have to find the right balance in our lives. It's not about eschewing the physical world. It's about making it work for us, while blessing and appreciating the environment and the bodies that make this 3D existence possible. By using our god-given gifts of wisdom, discernment, love, and intelligence—and activating those gifts by speaking up and being bold—we disarm the dark forces, my friends. We do it by being Our Selves. By claiming Our True Selves. By simply Being The Light.

CHAPTER 6

M'ama Non-M'ama

M'ama, non m'ama. Why do I know this phrase? Because it is the stupid name of a fancy, schmancy Italian jewelry line, whose *other* line I covet, that's why. And what does it mean? It sure *sounds* like the "To be or not to be" of mothering, but in fact, "m'ama non m'ama" means "she loves me, she loves me not." In Italian.

To be or not to be a mother. That is the question. I always assumed I would be one. I was married for a while in my late-twenties, early-thirties, and I wanted a kid, but not with the kid I was married to. I kept waiting for him to grow up. Didn't happen. He's now fathered some other broad's kid, but that's her business. He was baby enough for me.

I bought baby clothes when I was married because I just knew I'd be having kids. I hated that other, actually *pregnant* people got to buy stuff for their babies. So, I wasn't pregnant yet. That would change. Frustrated, I put a onesie on my fat cat, Chrissie. She sat there like a stuffed potato propped up on the couch, holding still for the camera. I now use flannel baby blankets to line my dog's carrier. Perhaps I should use the pacifiers to cork my wine bottles?

My collection of baby clothes grew as my marriage disintegrated. Since the guests of honor were dear friends, I chose to host both a bridal and a baby shower in my home as my relationship imploded, a profoundly difficult experience. After my separation, I pulled away from the married folk I'd hung out with during my marriage. It's not so fun to be in a group of couples when you're a single (and your ex was immediately re-coupled). I dropped off the face of the earth and made new friends, hanging out with artists, night owls, and other disenfranchised folk who were single and non-mommied. My mother experienced the same damn thing when my dad died. She was brutally booted out of her marital social circle. This time, I outed myself.

My parents had an ideal marriage in that not only did they love each other, but they liked and respected each other. They were partners. Dad went to work every day, Mom ran the home and took great care of my sister and me. She saw to it that we got the best academic and arts education New York City had to offer. Dad often told Mom that she should do more for herself, not just for us. He was probably right. After he died the same was true. She focused on us, putting an incredible amount of pressure on me (I can't speak for my sibling). I believe Mom's lack of healthy, happy enjoyment of her own life contributed to her early demise.

My heart went out to my mom, having to raise two kids by herself. She neither remarried nor dated again. "No man can hold a candle to him," she always said.

Even under the best of circumstances, you can't guarantee there'll be two parents around to follow through with raising your tiny humans. Both of mine ended up dead. Happens. I had more time with Mom than Dad, and even with a nine year spread between me and my big sister (effectively making us both only children) my mom had a hell of a hard time being a single parent. Parenting is challenging when you have two devoted parents and the luxury of two extended families. I had neither. I *never* wanted to be a single parent. And because Mom was 42 when she gave birth to me, I vowed to be a young mom. Not that there was anything wrong with my mom, except that she ended up dead. There seemed to be some correlation between old and dead. On the other hand, my father died in a non-age-related accident at 47. Life.

Now I know my parents were great in part *because* they were older. There's much to recommend the more seasoned adult as a parent. To generalize, they are calmer. Wiser. On the other hand, well, they're just not as *young*. Can't get around that one. But is young so great?

Having lost my dad at age five, I wanted to get married at 18 (to whom I don't know) and start reproducing in my 20s. This couldn't have been farther from my life's actual trajectory than ice from an oven. Having been foiled with a crappy first marriage, then saddled with extra helpings of "life lessons" as I toiled along my path with various and sundry "dating experiments," the years marched by. My childhood dream of a happy home, marriage, and family life was drifting farther and farther away.

I was frustrated. Angry. How do you fight your own karma? Could I yell at God, or would She yell back? Where did I lodge my karmic complaints and was mediation possible? I was off to a slow start as it was. I was such a late bloomer sexually that I actually had a spirit guide tell me to get laid, and by any means necessary. It's not often that the heavens open up and tell you to "get busy." I was a tough nut to crack. But here I am now. Cracked.

When I tell people that I believe I will have kids naturally, some of them say, "Well, what are you waiting for?"

I reply calmly, "The father of the children."

"You don't need a man for that."

"Oh yes, I do." A good marriage means more to me than having kids, but I've always trusted they would both "just come." I'm in my forties now and neither is here. Forget the clock. I'm only glad I didn't know this was how things would pan out when I was younger. Would have put me in a bad mood.

My parents raised me a Theosophist and I am firmly entrenched in metaphysics, spirituality, reincarnation, karma—you name it, I'm on it. Having lost both my parents before the age of 22, I sought out psychic, channeled, and mediumistic readings for spiritual guidance and to re-establish contact with my folks. If I hadn't, I would have no semblance of family life at all.

Back in the days when I was *beyond* massively-profoundly-depressed, I received the most beautiful channeled readings from the spirit of Milarepa, a Tibetan poet and saint who meant nothing to me at the time. He was only as good as the info he coughed up. The info was solid gold (and poetic, to boot). I still refer back to those readings as events that he hinted at continue to unfold decades later. He knew me and my family inside and out. The person who "hosted" Milarepa did not know me, so you can't attribute the wisdom to chicanery. Now I know Milarepa was a way cool Tibetan poet and saint (the facts remain the same, only now, I care).

My almost-dead grandmother came through the ethers in one of my readings (sort of like making a phone call from the airport while you're waiting for your flight). She told me to "Stay put!"

Milarepa warned me that I had a strong death wish and that I was passively suicidal. This depressed me even more than I was already depressed. It was true, though I hadn't seen it. I just thought I was gloomy, unmotivated, and fucked. Nana promised me that I would be a mother someday. Big frickin' deal. I was 23, single, and the most important person in my life, my mother, had died a year prior, the day before Mother's Day (digging the knife in *just* a little deeper. My father died near Father's day. They knew how to make an impression).

I couldn't have cared less about being a parent at that time and certainly didn't need reassurance. Eons later I'm tapping my fingers and wondering when, exactly, this dog and pony show is gonna get going. Now I know why Nana promised. Bitch owes me a baby.

I envied my married-with-kids friends. I perceived them as "normal," having security, warmth, and company. It never occurred to me that some of my friends might have been jealous of me (either consciously or unconsciously) over the years because I am unencumbered, untethered, footloose, and fancy free. My time is my own, to write, tap dance, play with my pets, read a book, write a book, drink, listen to loud music, and nap. When I have the occasional cigarette I sit in my stairwell and blow smoke at the "No Smoking" sign. I am a free agent.

Years ago I got a mysterious letter in the mail. It was from Massachusetts. I didn't know anyone from the town and was perplexed. "Who the hell lives there? What is this?" I tried to fathom the secret to this mystery, scrutinizing the handwriting, the date stamp, the address. When I turned the letter over I exclaimed, "Oh, for fuck's sake."

Hand printed on the back it said, "The mother to be is registered at Buy, Buy, Baby."

"Goddammit!" I said out loud (and at work) "this is not an invitation, THIS IS A BILL!" I didn't even know who was pregnant and I had to buy her a present? The mother to be turned out to be one of the cadre of friends from my married days that I was no longer in touch with. She met her husband in my living room. They had a big beautiful wedding. Somewhere. After my divorce. I didn't go.

I had spoken to this gal at Christmas. She had invited me (and my ex, thanks a lot) to their Christmas party. I did not attend, for obvious reasons, but she had ample opportunity to tell me about her five months' pregnancy at that time. She refrained. I was outraged at being informed of her pregnancy by a stranger from Massachusetts. If I'm not a close enough friend to tell me yourself that you're pregnant, then why are you inviting me to your shower? I let her know how hurt I was and asked her why she didn't tell me at Christmas when she had the chance.

"I didn't want to hurt your feelings," she said.

First of all, she was assuming it *would* have hurt my feelings. Second, she was inviting me to the frickin' baby shower. At what point is it less "painful" for me to know about her impending motherhood? When they invited me for dinner?

"Oh, by the way, can you swing by the store and pick up some diapers?"

I did not attend the shower and I did not send a gift. I did visit the couple and their kid when he was about a year old. Mom was wary about who and what I now was, the lurking divorcée with a low social profile. Would I hate her kid? Would her kid hate me? I was relaxed and didn't pounce, so he came to me. We got along great.

The mother said, "I can't believe how good you are with him."

Shocking, I know, that someone who has a few social skills might know how to apply them to a small person. Animals like me. Kids like me. Whether or not I like them is another matter. It all depends on the upbringing. When I meet a well-behaved dog, cat, or child, the heavens open up and the angels sing. How many well-behaved adults do you know, for that matter?

I also find the mommy (I'm sorry, the nanny) culture fairly nauseating in this city (Nueva York). Nannies, nannies, nannies and nary a mommy in sight. Often Mommy is clad in Prada, jewels, and fuck-me shoes to prove she's still fuckable. Jackie O. did it well and yet she was a class act. She didn't walk around trying to catch the attention of film crews. In fact, as we well know, her behavior was in direct opposition to that cause. Everyone is so busy trying to "look good" and "do it all." I wonder if they do anything well. Do they spend time with their kid? I witness infants staring at iPhones, the new de facto babysitter at restaurants. I observe grandparents with their spawn's spawn on the bus. The kid stares at video games and Grandma stares straight ahead. Do they talk to each other? Lots of folk can't even maintain eye contact.

Parenting is undeniably hard work. The only way I will consider it is if I am with a fit partner, by which I mean someone who takes incredibly good care of *me*. Having been the "nice one" in all my relationships, I look forward to the day when I can reliably and happily count on a man's love and loyalty. My father was one of those men, true blue, loving, gentle, sweet, and strong. I've never heard a bad thing about him from anyone. The only crappy thing he ever did was die when I was five. I can't even hold that against him. He was special. Special men may be rare, but I only need one more.

I always promised myself when I had kids there would be no "Barney" in my home and that I would blast

Prodigy from the sound system. I'm not giving in to baby crap. The fact that my home is filled with dog and cat toys is a totally separate issue. In my parents' day the home was not filled with toys. The home was filled with grownups and grownup stuff. If you played with your toys you had to put them back in your room when you were finished. My cat and dog do not have their own room. They also don't have hands.

If I were to talk about my frustration at not having kids, I would also have to include my frustration at not having a mate, something I never thought I wouldn't have. I believe he's out there but I cannot make him simply "materialize," can I? "Pour reconstituted husband in glass, add wine, swirl, and sip!" I've done online dating (blcch) and all I can say is that I am intermittently a slut and a nun. I'm in a nun phase right now.

I'd like to prove them wrong, all the naysayers that say, "You have to do this," (go online to meet someone) and "You can't do that," (have a baby naturally after 50). I say I can and I will. First of all, it ain't over till it's over. I've survived so well and so long that some of my friends are now getting divorced (this includes the "buy, buy, baby" couple). I'm ahead of the game here. My wounds are healed. I don't have kids (a dating complication to be sure). Also, people do have babies later in life. They always have. They used to be called "change of life babies." Just when you thought you were done reproducing, there you are reproducing. I, in fact, was just such a surprise. My parents had my sister when they were 33 and while they wanted more kids, none came. They gave up hoping. Nine years later I appeared at the front door.

A friend's mom was 44 at her birth, another friend got pregnant at 47 (and miscarried, thank god—her boyfriend was a Godzilla-scale nightmare), my chiropractor's patient gave birth at 48...and Sarah from the bible, how old was she? 100? 200? Don't tell me it can't happen.

The fact of the matter is I don't want kids. I want a family. And a family starts with a solid, loving, and secure relationship with my partner. If I had to choose, I'd pick a partner over a kid. I want that relationship. The one I've never had. Oh, I've dabbled with some doozies over the decades. I don't want to be too mean, so I'll just say I got "the experience I needed." But I want a partner, best friend, a guy I'm comfortable with and who's relaxed with me. Someone I can build a life with. With *this* person I would consider having a child. If it's in the cards, as I believe it is, you better believe I'll be writing about the Immaculate Conception and miraculous birth. I'm not interested in test-tube babies, hormones, shots, and petri-dish progeny. I believe in making babies the good old-fashioned way, and if my mystery partner and I can't make that work, then so be it. I eat well, look young, exercise, and am in great shape. I also believe in miracles and acts of god, so what's the problem?

Some years ago I was asked in a channeling session if I was being the kind of parent I wanted to be to myself. I thought long and hard about that. Our parents set patterns in motion but it is we who maintain and prolong them. How was I parenting myself? My mother was fairly intense and critical. She loved me to pieces but the stress of losing both her parents early *and* her husband, well, I sympathize, but she took it out on me. I've learned over the years to be kinder and gentler to myself, more loving, patient, and nurturing. For this mother's day, I bought myself stuff that one typically buys one's mother, a lovely plush robe and pretty slippers.

I've mothered myself for years, nurturing the lonely child. Now I honor my Mother Self. I am a "hole in one" and whole in one, both Madonna and Child.

The process of turning my life around has been long and arduous. But I have results to show. I'm fabulous now. I'm happy, complete, and still want a mate, a new home, and maybe a kid or two. Though at times I think about the amount of work involved in having a baby and I'm plain grateful to have only me, my dog, and cat to take care of. It took an annoying husband to bring me to this level of appreciation of solitude and self. My home is my castle and I bask in its peace. I like me. There's no better place to start.

CHAPTER 7

Still Waters

I wanted a boyfriend. But I had three cats, which can be a little daunting to a guy, so I got rid of one. Oh, I didn't kill him myself. I hired a professional. Well, not such a good one. She had a really rough time killing him.

All right, I'm kidding. I'm kidding! But one of my three cats was very ill, and I had to make that terrible, terrible decision to put him out of his misery. The young vet on duty gave him "the shot." The only problem was—he didn't die. Since he was still breathing, I nervously commented on this to the doctor, and she gave him a second shot. Usually, this fun-filled activity takes seconds to work, but ten minutes later, my cat was lying on his side, smoking a cigarette. The doctor ran out of the room and returned with a third shot.

"This is to relax him," she said.

"It seems to me he's pretty relaxed," I said. "Can you get something to kill him?"

She gave him a third shot. He started reciting the periodic table.

My cat had been sick since he was a kitten; I figured he was on his 13th or 14th life by now. I wasn't in a particularly buoyant mood, given the day's activity, putting my beloved, giant tabby Sam down, and the fact that the dreadful deed was not "taking" for some freakish reason was doubling and tripling the trauma. I kept tearfully kissing him goodbye. And he kept not dying.

I was used to doing brutal stuff like this by myself. (I'd put down three cats before Sam, and I always hold and comfort them until they've passed.) However this time, my friend Andrea kindly joined me at the vet's office.

"My god, he's like Rasputin!" she said.

Rasputin was the Russian mystic and advisor to Czar Nicholas and Alexandra. In an attempt to do away with him, his enemies poisoned his favorite cream puffs but he didn't die. So they stabbed him. He didn't like this at all so he ran away. Rasputin's tormentors chased after him, shot him, and threw his body into the freezing river. The magic combination of freezing, drowning, stabbing, shooting, and poison finally did the trick for Rasputin. My cat was four shots to the wind when he gave up the ghost. I dubbed Sam "Raspussy."

Though depressed, I was now down to two cats and free and clear to date. I went online and whom did I meet? A widower. Happily married for years, his wife had died of cancer. I thought it indelicate to ask him when she had passed. I figured, he was up and running on a dating website, a respectable period of mourning must have elapsed. We emailed a little, and things warmed up. I jokingly signed one of my emails to him Lily Von Schtupp, Madeleine Kahn's sexy character in *Blazing Saddles*. He responded as Frau Bleucher, the old hag with facial warts who made horses scream in *Young Frankenstein*.

This took me aback. I gasped, "Why'd he pick a woman to respond as? And an ugly one at that?"

A friend chastised me. "Come *on*, lighten up! You're being too picky."

I was emphatic. "Oh, no. Oh, *no, no, no, no, no*. Mark my words, my friend, there is something very, *very* wrong here. I gave him a juicy visual to work with. Madeleine Kahn was hot in that garter belt. I don't want to date Frau Bleucher!"

I met him anyway because, let's be honest, most of my dates ended up as research for my performances, and now, my writing.

The guy was vegetarian, yet he was wearing leather pants. He was six-foot-two so that was what, four dead cows wrapped around his ass, but he wouldn't eat one? During dinner he said, "Wow! Where'd you get those boots?"

I froze. That is girl talk, not dude talk. Since I didn't respond in a timely fashion he quipped, "What, Parade of Shoes?"

I joked back, deadpan, "No, Payless."

Most guys would say, "Nice boots," if they admired them on you, not inquire as to *where* they were procured. I could only conclude that he wanted a pair for himself. And as if I didn't already have enough evidence to present my closing arguments, he pulled me to him when we walked by NYU and whispered, "Did you see that beautiful boy over there? He was sooo androgynous!"

I was at a loss as to why his personal ad stated, "Man seeking Woman." It was 2005, this was New York City, and he worked in the theater. How much easier could *we* make it for *him* to come out? On top of that, his wife had died an unseemly three months prior. His ad should have read "Confused vegetarian seeks nice boots and young, androgynous male. Wife freshly dead." He showed me a photo of her. While pretty, she was flat chested and had a pixie haircut. He married Peter Pan. Case closed.

I was disheartened and, when I was depressed, I used to watch forensics shows to cheer me up. I may have been down, but at least I wasn't dead, dismembered, and decomposing. It put my misery in perspective. I had one up on these people. I had the great good sense not to date serial killers, just strange, gay widowers. In fact, after watching the shows I was relieved I was single. I was still alive, in one piece, merely depressed, but safe and sound on my lovely couch. My spirits weren't high but my vitals were strong.

One particularly "uplifting" segment on Court TV featured the story of a raped and murdered teenaged girl in South Carolina. The police asked her classmates to volunteer blood samples to rule out suspects. It turned out that one of the volunteers *was* the killer. The boy was absolutely baffled how they knew it was him from a measly blood test. The sheriff said, "Your DNA was a one in a million match, son."

The good-looking high school boy queried skeptically, "What's DNA?"

He probably thought it was a venereal disease. "Doc told me I had the herpes and the clap, not no dang DNA. Shoot, they tricked me!"

After Frau Bleucher, I met another guy online. We spoke on the phone. Most would agree that you try to put your best foot forward when you're getting to know someone. This guy said right off the bat he thought the human race was doomed. Now I get a little down sometimes, but overall, I'm a pretty positive person. To say the human race is doomed, I dunno, that was a little dark for me and I told him so.

He protested, "I am not a pessimist. Well, not in my *personal* life." So, he's *personally* happy as he bounds off to work in the morning, Starbucks in hand, but he thinks it's a distinct possibility that the world might explode sometime after lunch? Yeah, real upbeat. Sure.

Then he went on about Donald Trump. "Blah, blah, blah…that's why he's a millionaire, and I'm a pauper."

A pauper? He neglected to mention in his dating profile that he was a pauper. In fact my profile specifically stated, "Please, no paupers…"

When he asked if I had any animals at home, I told him I'd gotten rid of my husband, I only had the two cats now. And why did he say *animals*, not *pets*? I asked if he had any "animals."

He said, "Oh no, my apartment is way too tiny (of course, he's a pauper) and they're too much work."

Regarding my ex-husband, I had to agree about the work, but the cats? They're no trouble at all. What do they do? They look. They look away. They sit. They lounge. They loiter. They're vaguely mobile décor.

"Well, I *love* animals," I said defensively.

He sassed back, "So do I, just not in the home, and certainly, *certainly* not in the bedroom."

Since I slept with my "animals," I didn't respond.

He then proceeded to hang himself, delivering the one-two punch. "Look, I wash my nether region every night before I go to bed. And I expect the same of anyone else in my bed."

Is it possible he said that? He *washes his crotch nightly* and saw fit to tell me, a potential date, the details of these nightly ablutions? What could he *possibly* say next to sweep me off my feet, that he jerked off while sniffing Mr. Clean? The air crackled with tension.

"My cats are cleaner than some of the men I've slept with," I retorted. "And I'm so tidy that my friend David observed that my kitty litter was clean enough to eat off of."

This conversation was not going well. He upped the ante. "I'm not religious, but even *The Bible* says you shouldn't sleep with animals."

"*That* was a liturgical reference to my *ex-husband*," I retorted.

But I'm thinking to myself, this guy really, really just doesn't want any pussy in bed. And that can be arranged.

He continued. "I don't know if this is a deal breaker for you, but I draw the line at cat ass in the bed."

Cat ass. He spoke the very words. No cat ass in the bed. Not even *my* bed. My cats. Was this a deal breaker for me? How about the whole frickin' *conversation* was a deal breaker?

I hadn't even met this guy and he was already discussing his *nether region* and my cats' asses. Impertinence and inappropriateness doesn't even begin to cover what was wrong with this dude. I said, "Lemme tell you something, you pessimistic, genital-rinsing pauper. When I'm not getting dick, I like a little CAT ASS in my bed!!! Keeps me warm at night."

And just then, right on cue, I swear to God, my cat Wilbur walked up to me on the couch and presented his precious posterior like it was some sort of special gift, which I suppose it was (to him). I couldn't resist. I had no choice but to put the phone up to his little cat ass. I said, "You know what? You two talk. You have a lot in common."

When I told my cousin Genia about this latest dating debacle, she said with her New Yawk accent, "Couldn't he just say he showers at night?"

Next up to bat were two guys who were polar opposites. So much so that I was convinced I had to sleep with both of them in order to find my perfect match. One was a guy I met at a New Age class. He was a performer, and I bumped into him from time to time at auditions or New

Age events. I thought he was attractive, but he was over the top. A big, Hungarian bear of a guy, he once picked me up by my ass. Just pulled me to him, grabbed my ass, and picked me up. I took it all in stride, but it did occur to me that he was a sex fiend. He took my number, but never asked me on a date. He'd call at 11 p.m. and say, "What are you doing?"

I'd reply, "Going to *bed.*"

Or, he'd call and joke with me, but it was always about sex. I mentioned to him that if he called earlier in the day, or actually made plans with me, we might be able to get together. Sometime.

A year and a half later, he picked me up in his car. It wasn't perfect, but I hadn't had sex in two years, and I needed to get out of the house. He told me to wear heels and a mini skirt. I told him to go fuck himself. I also told him I was just getting over a rash. I'd been anxious and had hives. He was mortified. He said, "You mean, you mean we can't *hug*?"

I said we could *hug*. But I didn't really think he wanted to just *hug*.

He was all over me immediately and I didn't object. He was amazingly tender and a fantastic kisser. We kissed all over the East Village. I wasn't crazy about him but he was fun and I went with it. It was nice to be touched, especially after how tense I'd been.

I did notice, when his body was pressed up against mine, that while his breathing was irregular and he was getting sweaty, I couldn't discern any activity "down south" if you catch my drift. I thought, "Maybe he's being polite?"

But he *wasn't* polite, he was a pig, so that made no sense. At any rate, he kept kissing me on every street corner and park bench and frankly, I was exhausted. I just wanted to go to bed. Alone. He drove me home and started kissing me. Again. He said he wanted to come upstairs and *hug*. I said, "The way you *hug*, a girl could get pregnant," and departed.

He called but I wasn't interested. He was too exhausting.

Two weeks later, after a date with his polar opposite, an extremely uptight, overly apologetic musician, and *terrible* kisser who rivaled Howard Hughes in his oddness, I started re-thinking the Hungarian Hugger and what a good kisser he was. My friends encouraged me, "Just get laid. Seriously."

He and I spoke again. I said, "How about dinner?"

He said, "What are you making?"

I snapped, "Wrong answer."

He responded, "That wasn't an answer, it was a question."

"Wrong answer and wrong question!" I retorted and hung up.

He was a big dog. He wanted to hump, get scratched and fed. It was an offer I could definitely refuse. Two more months went by, I was still going through my dry patch and still thinking about the tight squeezes and soft kisses. I broke down when he invited me out for hot cocoa at 11 p.m. on a school night. I declined, sighed, and countered in resignation, "Why don't you just come over."

I was never gonna get a real date out of this guy. He arrived in ten minutes. He brought a sandwich from the deli. He kissed me passionately. He ate his sandwich and offered me a bite.

"Uh...no thanks."

We kissed some more. Things got heated and our clothes started coming off. When he got down to his underwear my jaw dropped. There was no activity below the Mason-Dixon line. I inquired gently, "Did you leave something in the car?"

You could have knocked me over with a feather. Where was my sex fiend? Where was the pervert? I was so convinced this guy was trouble, I never suspected in a million years it would be this kind of trouble. But there was more. Not only did things never get fully "up to speed" shall we say, but he liked to talk dirty. Really dirty. I'd never been with a dirty talker before. It was the most ridiculous juxtaposition of behaviors. Here he was talking like Long Dong Silver with no artillery. If you're going to talk like that, you better have a movie to follow the trailer.

But I was a good sport. A really good sport. He called me a puta. This was hysterical. I'm a nice white girl from Manhattan who hadn't been laid in years. Then he slapped me. I knew he'd want to do something with my ass, and I was glad it was just that. But I giggled at that, too.

Then, when I got on top of him, pretending that everything was fine while looking askance at what we were working with, he looked down and said, "You want to fuck this?"

I winced and whispered, "Yeah?"

"Yeah?" he insisted.

I eked out a slightly more audible, "Yeah."

He pushed again, "YEAH?"

I yelped, "Yeah! Yeah! Yeah!"

For goodness sake. It was bad enough I had to pretend I had something to work with, but he wanted me to sing the praises of his non-working number, too? Why call attention to what is simply not there?

I felt like Lisa Lupner, Gilda Radner's dorky character on *Saturday Night Live*. Bill Murray played her geeky boyfriend Tod. (Remember, he pounded "nuggies" on her head and commented on her bewitching scent, Vick's VapoRub?) Every time this guy said or did something I felt like snorting, "TOD!" and pushing Lisa's imaginary goofy glasses back up my nose. I said, instead, to Huggie Bear, that no one had ever spanked me or talked dirty to me before (which was true).

He asked knowingly (as if it explained everything), "Is that why you were smiling so much?"

I nodded my head up and down solemnly while suppressing yet another laugh. He really did just want to hug, after all.

After that shocking episode, I decided that appearances being deceiving, I needed to sleep with the weird musician on the theory that maybe he wasn't as geeky as he seemed. Perhaps his still waters ran deep. We never made it to bed. I discovered that some still waters are really…just…still.

Normally when I went to my gynecologist she'd ask me what I was using for birth control and I'd glumly say, "Nothing."

She raised an eyebrow accusingly. "Why nothing?"

I explained, "Because I'm not having sex!"

My dry spells tended to last a while. I had my yearly gynecological visit shortly after "Mr. Kiss and Run." I had Doc and her assistant heaving with laughter when I told them about my experience with the pornographic under-performer.

Not long after I met a new guy, and as I lay on his bed, fully clothed, with just a touch of a hand to an arm, I noticed out of the corner of my eye that there *was* something down south, and it was fully animated. This was music to my eyes, and an invitation I could not refuse. I also received an auspicious omen from his lava lamp, which produced a distinctly priapic apparition. I took this as a sign from the gods that I was to proceed with abandon. Add to this that he was covered in dog hair and I was covered in cat hair, and, well, you can imagine the particular magic that we made.

CHAPTER 8

Iced Coffee

Do you know what tort reform is? Most people don't even know what a tort is, and I was one of them. It is a "wrong." Someone does something bad, evil, or negligent and this event or behavior affects you adversely. It fucks you up. In this country, this used to mean that you could seek legal redress since most fucker-uppers don't admit to their wrongdoing, let alone apologize and offer to make it right. Hence the Seventh Amendment and our right to trial by a jury of our peers. If people are irresponsible and hurt us, we have a right to seek reprisal.

I am so big on personal responsibility that I too was one of those people who felt that this country was filled with "frivolous lawsuits." The most famous of those being the McDonald's "hot coffee" case. An old lady bought hot coffee at Mickey D's in Albuquerque, New Mexico, and it burned the shit out of her. Awww...Come *on*, old lady, we say! Hot coffee is *supposed* to be...hot. What a ninny. What a sissy. Put that little old lady in a nursing home where the Sanka and Cremora are nice and *lukewarm,* safe like the bedrails and butterscotch pudding.

When I was interviewed for jury duty I was asked my opinion about frivolous lawsuits. I offered that there were many suits that were countless and baseless. My own father died (or was killed, depending on your perspective) at an airshow while simulating WWII dogfights in original planes. My mother was informed that the other pilot had put my dad in a bad spot and that she could sue. She chose not to, saying, "What good would it do? It won't bring your father back and I would have to relive the whole thing. And think how badly the other pilot must already feel about it."

Yes, we could have used the money. But I respect my mother's position. She was not litigious, she accepted her karma. And yes, she was very, very sad, upset, and tormented by my father's death. But why does someone always have to pay for our hurts? Sometimes life hurts and there's no one to blame. Are some people overly litigious? Sure. Are there lots and lots of frivolous lawsuits? Surprise answer—not as many as you think.

Turns out this whole "frivolous lawsuit" thing was a big put up job by the Bush administration and the Corporatocracy that's been running this U.S. of A. (fortunately, their contract was up in 2012, the power is returning again to The People). Rent the documentary *Hot Coffee*, and you'll find out exactly why and how the wool has been pulled over your eyes. Attorney Susan Saladoff made this film. Each of the four cases she explores involve egregious wrongs committed against the plaintiffs. In all four cases, the plaintiffs lost. Even the "hot coffee" old lady who was awarded $2.9 million in 1994 (her settlement was massively reduced, while her pain and suffering was not). Yes, Ladies and Gentlemen, you heard and read that right. Guess who won? McDonalds, Halliburton, the Chamber of Commerce, and some shit ob-gyn who had other hideous claims against her but which were never made public. The Corporatocracy has been pulling strings and manipulating lives right before our eyes.

So, Liebeck (little old lady) was 79 at the time of the incident, vibrant, and had a job up until the Mickey D's event. Never sued anyone before in her life. If this was a frivolous case, then she must be a frivolous woman and nothing in her past reflected or indicated that. It took but one thing to understand the gravity of her case: viewing photos of her wounds. They were absolutely *disgusting*. The flesh between her thighs was blackened from scabbing. These were third degree burns. I've suffered second and third degree burns from boiling water. All pain is rough (heck, even a paper cut or splinter is bad, right?) but I have particular sympathy for burn patients because burns produce an incessant, fiery pain that continues to, well...*burn*, for a long, long time. The fires brutally smolder as your body attempts to recover from the trauma. This little old lady required painful skin grafts from the outside of her thighs to repair the inside of her thighs and groin, so badly was she mutilated.

One of my college roommates suffered a similar burn in the same place from the same burning hot brown liquid. She sustained a large, ugly looking scar on her upper thigh. I was shocked at how big and bad her scar was. Didn't sue the dining hall or college, but I'm not aware that her thigh turned crusty and black, either. Liebeck got it bad.

Turns out this particular Mickey D's in Albuquerque had over 700 complaints about burns from scalding beverages (which were kept at 170-180 degrees, or was it 180-190?) Boiling is 212. Do you want a product which is practically cauldron-bubbling hot? That's not how I take my java, like lava. In fact, I frequently default to iced. The McDonald's employee who was depositioned said he was not only fine with the figure of 700 complaints but that he was actually "relieved" it wasn't bigger. This is a guy who's essentially "good" with the figure of "only" 58,282 dead American soldiers from the Vietnam War. After the lawsuit McDonalds dropped their standard holding temperature a whopping ten degrees.

The next case involved twin boys whose ob-gyn neglected to give an ultrasound when the mother reported that the babies had stopped moving in utero at 36 weeks. Doc satisfied herself with checking the heartbeat instead of spending the extra what, twenty minutes via sonogram ensuring that the fetuses had separate placentas. Five days later the problem remained. Mom went to the hospital and was told she needed an immediate caesarian. Her doctor showed up two hours later, ignoring the prescribed ten minute window for action as suggested by "immediate." One twin is perfect in every way. The other twin, who did not have his own placenta, had been deprived of oxygen (it all shunted to his brother) and came out with every mental and physical handicap that you can imagine.

Turns out Doc had a crappy malpractice record, but this information was not allowed in court. The boy was awarded $5.6 million to ensure that he would have adequate care for the rest of his life. But due to Bush's tort reform and medical malpractice caps, that was reduced to $1.25 million. Not enough to care for the lifetime of this child. So Medicaid pays the rest, instead of the doctor responsible for this egregious oversight. With any luck, she's probably still wreaking havoc on other unwitting patients.

Oliver Diaz is a judge in Tennessee. Since Bush's Cabal was busy buying up judges that would benefit the Corporatocracy, they tried hard to oust Diaz, an honest judge who did not defer to Master Money. Diaz actually won a re-election campaign despite the lies and incredible odds against him broadcast by his opponents, all paid for by the Chamber of Commerce (sounds like a government agency, does it not? It's not. It's private, like the Federal Reserve. Neither benefits We The People). Once Diaz won, he was indicted for bogus fraud (of which he was acquitted) then bogus tax fraud (of which he was also acquitted). This case was so fiendish that John Grisham wrote about it in his blockbuster, *The Appeal*. Though Diaz was innocent, the Cabal was successful in getting him off the bench for a full three years. Which means they kept earning money hand over fist since justice was never meted out under their crooked cronies' "judicial" watch. Diaz now works for The Justice Project, which seeks to exonerate wrongfully convicted individuals through DNA testing and reforming the criminal justice system.

The last case involved Jamie Leigh Jones, a young gal from Houston who went to work for Halliburton subsidiary KBR. I'm very close to calling it Russia's infamous and brutal KGB, and for good reason. Even KBR's crappy corporate logo is an ominous blood red. Jamie was 19 when her mom got sick and Jamie needed to find a job to help support her family. She worked for KBR in Houston first then was "invited" to go over to Iraq. She was assured she had more chance of being injured in her car over here than she had of getting wounded over there. She was promised housing in female quarters.

She arrived in Iraq and was put in a trailer filled with men who catcalled and harassed her. She complained. She was told she'd get used to it. She "awoke" one day to find herself bleary, sick, bloody, and in massive pain. She had been drugged, brutally gang raped vaginally and anally, and required reconstructive surgery. One of her rapists (they were all co-workers) was brazen enough to hang around on her bed, waiting for her to wake up. Once she started to realize what had happened to her, she was imprisoned in a shipping container for several days. She begged and screamed to be released. Someone finally took pity on her and gave her his cell phone. She called home, her mom got the government involved, and she was sent home. Since she had signed a standard arbitration clause (as many of us have, usually without knowing it) with KBR, she had signed her rights to legal redress away. When an "arbitrator" is called in, it is done so by the corporation, so the arbitrator is beholden to his employer. I guess Jamie never figured her new employer would sanction her harassment, drugging, rape, and imprisonment. Just one of the "perks" of working for KBR/Halliburton that they never bothered to mention.

The fine print we get mailed with our credit cards (that we all throw out because it's too small and boring to read, a fact they rely on) says essentially, "new terms: you agree to arbitrate in a dispute with us, when you make another purchase with your credit card, it means you have agreed to these terms." No one agreed to the terms because no one read them. It's a boondoggle. The bank wins 99 out of 100 times, because the bank pays the arbitrator. The arbitrator is *not* impartial.

Senator Al Franken came to Jamie Leigh Jones' rescue. He got some mandatory arbitration law overturned, leaving room for the possibility of litigation. Jamie Leigh Jones has received no legal redress via civil or federal court. Are you surprised? When up against Halliburton? The house always wins. Apparently it is standard business practice for KBR's female employees to be drugged, raped, and sodomized. She was sent over there as a sacrifice, a sex slave, against her knowledge and will. My friend Bill said this case was used as the basis of a *The

Good Wife episode. Thank god this story got some coverage somewhere. It sure didn't in the news.

Now, to that, let me add this. I knew someone in Upstate New York who bought a pricey new home in a depressed area. She was a target within weeks or months of a lawsuit filed by a contractor who claimed he "tripped on her carpet" or some shit. On the surface, it seemed an obvious attempt to extort money from this rich broad. I don't know the details of the case, if there was any actual merit (I'm assuming not) or how it turned out.

And this. A "handicapped" fellow on my street corner accepts donations in his paper cup. I assume he does well as he's kept his post for sixteen years, but I can't swear that he needs the wheelchair. I heard a ruckus as I approached the corner and saw this business guy looking all upset and staring at his hand. There was no blood. Apparently a suburban vehicle had sideswiped him as he was crossing the street. Let's assume the car was in the wrong. An ambulance pulled up. The fire department was at the light, waiting to come investigate. The cops were there. Tommy, the guy in the chair says, "You see that? Now *that's* a lawsuit! Why that can't be me? Why?"

I had no pity for Tommy wanting to make money that way and I had no pity for the suit. He seemed to be "acting" hurt, as opposed to "being" hurt. Now, did his finger hurt? Maybe. Was it broken? Who knows? Did he sustain other injuries? Didn't look like it. He seemed perfectly fine to me.

I, on the other hand, was mowed down by a suburban vehicle years ago at an intersection in New York City at night. The box of homemade Christmas cookies I was carrying went flying. I didn't have health insurance. The guy in the car was petrified. He had knocked me over, and it hurt like hell. Fortunately, I was wearing a winter coat that protected me somewhat (my guardian angel was also clearly pulled away from dinner for an assist). I was able to slowly get up with the driver's help. He offered me a lift to where I was going, his business card (he was an optometrist with a foreign accent) and $40. I was pretty fucked up. But I'm not litigious. Maybe I was an asshole. My body ached for days, probably weeks (it was a while ago). Obviously, nothing was broken, but I needed several trips to my chiropractor, who said "Well, you lost about two inches." (The body contracts with pain/shock/accidents).

I'm only five feet tall, so every inch counts. Fortunately, my recovery over time included retrieving my two inches. But I felt like my mom did. Why sue? I was okay. Mostly. Sort of. The guy was genuinely mortified (and he was totally in the wrong since I had the light). Could I have called him and asked for more money? Sure. Could I have sued? Yes. I didn't. And it would have been a pain in the ass for me. I shelled out the money to go to my healer and yes, I had pain and suffering. Suburban vehicles are considerably bigger than my five-foot frame. Had I lost my ability to walk, it would have been another story altogether.

I had another "run in" with a car while rollerblading. A cab door opened in front of me and knocked me to the ground. This was not good. We were right in front of The Plaza Hotel and the couple in the cab stepped over my body to get to the hotel without ever looking down at me, let alone asking if I was all right. To quote Bea Arthur from the fabulous 1970's TV show, *Maude*, "God will get them."

The Indian cab driver was petrified and hysterical, "Lady! Get up! Lady! Get up! Lady!"

A crowd gathered. I usually get up to make sure that I can. Then a Jamaican cab driver jumped to my defense.

"NO, MAN, (that was me) DON'T GET UP! Don't get up, man! Stay on the ground. I'll get an ambulance."

Still uninsured, I didn't want the ambulance. How would I pay for it? I managed to get up, badly hurt, but vaguely functional. I hobbled down the stairs to meet a friend for a movie at the Plaza. I could barely walk and was in brutal pain. My "friend," irritated by my tardiness, stepped over me to get popcorn. I left minutes later, took a cab home, and never spoke to my "friend" again.

And recently, at lunch, I drank an iced cappuccino. I regretted this purchase. While the coffee idea had first appealed when I ordered it on a blistering NYC summer day, by the time it arrived, I was kinda stuffed from my sandwich and water. There was a lot of milk in the iced beverage, and though the drink wasn't large, I felt *bloated* for the rest of the afternoon. My stomach was distended. Indeed, I was uncomfortable. A perfectly pleasant lunch had turned into something ominous with my stomach disagreeably gurgling. I contemplated my options as I roamed the sweltering streets of Manhattan seeking relief, but did I need redress? I could not escape the physical distress. Who would I blame? The restaurant? The waitress? (she was an enabler). I pouted, seeking shade and reprieve, and, could it be, revenge? Grumbling and sweating, I eventually walked it off and decided not to sue the cafe.

What's my point? *I'm not litigious.* That businessman in the suit on my corner was a pussy with a boo-boo on his finger. Maybe it *was* bruised. Boo, hoo. The guy in the wheel chair is a fool to want a real accident (or rather, a bullshit one) so he can sue someone for his version of "easy money." I don't want to sue anyone. But damn it, if someone truly hurts or maligns me, I want the right to kick the shit out of them in court. Irresponsible people must be made to pay so that they stop hurting other people. There are plenty of sociopaths out there. Many of them are Corporations. Corporations do not have feelings, just bottom lines. They don't care if people are hurt by their products or practices so long as they keep making money. And that's why we have to stand up to them.

Know your rights. Find your voice. Speak up. Even I was suckered in by this "frivolous lawsuit" crap. It's easy to be sandbagged by slick PR, advertising and propaganda. Hitler and Bush (or rather, Bush's handlers) were aces in this field. Don't be a sucker. Wake up. Look. Listen. Pay attention. Don't be brainwashed. Stand up for what is right. Take your power back. It's time we all do. The personal *is* political. What happens to you, or me, happens to all of us. WEAREALLONE.

CHAPTER 9

Twisted

I was serving breakfast to a cranky old man. Not the famous cranky old man I had just dated. Nor the controlling older man I had studied personal growth happily with for years then agreed to work for before quitting six weeks later and running to the emergency room for stress related symptoms on my last day. No, this was a *different* cranky old man. Rich. Powerful. And with a temper on him.

He liked three ounces of tomato juice in the morning. A full cup of black coffee. And half a white bagel, doughy center pulled out, the empty shell toasted well. How did I end up here, an adorable, well-educated, talented younger woman, serving breakfast to an irascible geezer in his office? I was asking myself the same question.

I was hired as a temp over the phone, the friend of a friend of an employee. They didn't even interview me in person. They needed a *body* and fast, someone breathing, and stolid enough to survive the old man's miserable moods.

I was sick of day jobs I didn't like. And I was sick of mean people, specifically, the difficult older man I'd recently dated who had an explosive temper. He yelled at me for touching his things and screamed violently at me for crimes such as using too much water in the shower. And I'd just worked briefly for a man who never raised his voice, but who quietly controlled a fearful empire, incessantly bearing down on his beleaguered and underpaid non-profit employees. My boss was 65, my beau was 70. This guy was 80. And was he ever moody. I wanted to punch him in the face before I ever met him.

I knew he was a son of a bitch going in. I could hear the *massive* stress in the voice of the gal who recruited me over the phone. I could hear him screaming at her in the background. But the hourly rate was very good, so my ear remained glued to the phone while I aurally witnessed the horrors in this gilded office. I was massively wary. But the stint was temporary. I could walk away from the firing squad if I wanted.

He used to run one of the biggest businesses in the world of its type. President, Chairman, and CEO. He was *almost* a billionaire, and it killed him that he wasn't. He'd be a coupla thousand, a coupla hundred thousand, or a few million shy of a billion each day. It wore on him. He was retired now and kept an office open to manage his investments. That's all he did—played with his money all day. And when I say play, I mean like a cat toying with its prey. I went in prepared to quit on a moment's notice.

I'd gotten good at that lately. After nearly five years, I quit a corporate job I hated (one of those big rotten financial companies that got bailed out) to work at a personal growth retreat in a bucolic setting. It seemed the potential answer to my prayers, doing meaningful work in a beautiful setting with people I loved and respected. That situation blew up in my face immediately so I returned to NYC six weeks later. I walked into a chic home goods store in Soho to browse and was spontaneously offered a sales position. The pay was low but the store was spacious and lovely. I quit a week later when I was sent to detention in the duvet section for talking with a colleague at ten a.m. when there were no customers around.

I felt like a wildcat that'd been freed from her cage. I'd allowed myself to stay stuck for years, in a bad marriage, then in clerical jobs. But I was on fire now. There was no pinning me down at a job I didn't like. I needed adventure. And I was determined to be happy.

Jury duty cropped up. My daily reward for doing jury duty was Thai food with beer for lunch (Manhattan's courts are by Chinatown). My "specialty" was coming back drunk for the voir dire. I used to care about jury duty. I actually yearned to be selected (this was when kickass Judge Leslie Crocker Snyder was presiding over one of the cases) but the lawyers never picked me, so I started letting it rip at lunch. One Tsingtao beer and I was gone.

And that's when this random call came through inviting me to work for Mr. Black, while I was strolling around the streets of Chinatown during jury duty lunch break on a sunny April day. His assistant called me; she was the friend of a friend who had recommended me. She sounded highly stressed and was *thinking* through clenched teeth. I couldn't even get her to focus on the questions I was asking because she was totally preoccupied by the old man snarling and spitting ominously at her back. "Rough environment?" I asked. She didn't answer, but I could feel her nod her assent over the phone.

When he ran his large corporation, Mr. Black had eight—count 'em, eight—assistants. He was now down to a paltry three. Having sold his business, his occupation now was micromanaging his money. He watched the market and his Bloomberg screens like a hawk. At the end of every day he wanted to know *to the penny* how much money was in each of his brokerage accounts. If he was down a dollar, he got irritated. I was to work for Scrooge.

People came and went from this office like people getting on and off the subway at rush hour. They quit or were fired, usually under highly dramatic circumstances. People who survived had steel stomachs and shattered nerves. Jane was his Primary Assistant, or Wife Number One, as I liked to call her, not to be confused with the boss's actual wife of fifty years, an equally cranky old woman.

Mary was Wife Number Two, Assistant to the Assistant. She was there but two weeks, fresh from a stint at Martha Stewart. When they hired her, they figured if she could handle Martha, she could handle Mr. Black. They were wrong. His previous primary assistant had been a soldier in the Israeli army. These were the prerequisites for working there. My last boyfriend taught me to handle a shotgun. I was perfect for the job.

I was Wife Number Three, Assistant to the Assistant to the Assistant. I hated it immediately and turned down their repeated requests for me to go full-time. I didn't even want to know how much it paid. Every day I left disgusted from witnessing the ongoing emotional carnage that smoldered like a hot bomb site. I told a few people on the QT, "You probably won't ever see me again. Nice working with you," since reserving the right never to return made working there daily palatable. Every night I left I shot my colleagues dire, meaningful looks.

If I returned in the morning, I was like the Phoenix bird, arisen from the ashes. Their faces lit up. "You're back!"

I started feeling like Fred from *Sanford and Son* when he feigned his myriad heart attacks, "This is the big one, Elizabeth, I can feel it! I'm comin', honey!"

I was not on the fence about working there. I was *dangling* from it, the fence itself rattling mightily from the ever present "human twister" that ravaged this Ninth Level of Dante's Inferno.

Mary was young and plus size. Mr. Black hated her. He hated her because she was simpering and because she was portly. Despite her time at Martha, Mary quickly turned red in the face and sweated in the presence of Mr. Black. Besides, she liked Martha. Jane, Wife Number One, was ninety pounds wet, but despite the regular, excoriating verbal attacks on her by Mr. Black, she had him wrapped around her little finger in her own twisted way. We all had our ways of surviving and we all had our reasons for being there. What were mine?

As it turned out Mr. Black was inclined favorably toward me since my anonymous hatred of him held some sort of appeal. I didn't kiss his ass. I wanted nothing to do with him. I avoided him at all costs, not out of fear, but contempt. He obviously found this intriguing.

When I was assigned the "scooping" and toasting of his morning bagel, I asked Jane how dark he liked it toasted.

She said, "Well."

When I presented my handiwork to Mr. Black he preemptively protested, "I only wanted a half!"

I pointedly pointed out the obvious. "It *is* a half."

He looked again and, wind taken out of his sails, said, "Oh."

I scooped and toasted that bagel so expertly that he requested the other half, a first in that office. What can I say? He liked my cooking. He was taking a cotton to me, much to my dismay. It occurred to me, as I stood over the trash in the kitchen, that eviscerating and toasting a grumpy old man's bagel just might not be a high point in my career. Besides, if you want your bagel scooped, why don't you just eat *toast*?

Mary, the heavy girl, was not as anticipatory as I and didn't inquire beforehand as to the level of darkness to which The Dark One's scooped out bagel should be toasted. When she brought it to him he railed, "Look at it! It doesn't even *look* toasted! *Can we cook these a little longer?!* MORON!!"

When he yelled everyone tensed up as the volcano smoked, smoldered, then started to spew molten lava. It didn't matter what you did (or didn't) do. If he was in a bad mood and you were in his line of fire, the bull's eye was on you.

But things really deteriorated with Wife Number Two when Mr. Black asked her for a large, twisty pretzel (a low fat staple in the office). She brought him the bag. I thought someone who'd worked for Martha and was familiar with the silver and china collection in the kitchen should know better than to bring the old man a plastic bag for him to reach into. He barked at her, "Get me a plate!"

She scurried back with a plate and two pretzels. "Here you are, Mr. Black."

Smoke blew out of his ears. *"Now let's get something straight here*!!!!" he bellowed, "When I ask for *one* pretzel, I want ONE, not TWO! You are trying to make me fat! If you don't stop this passive aggressive behavior, I'll be forced to dismiss you!"

Mary quit a week later and sued his ass. Her father worked in HR somewhere and Dad educated his progeny on her employee bill of rights. Mr. Black was a walking lawsuit. Mary's departure did not bode well for me, since there was now one less body between me and Mr. Black.

I was bumped up a notch to Wife Number Two, the buffer of the nervous youngster no longer protecting me. The Evil Eye of Sauron was directed toward me, as on Frodo wearing the Ring. Sauron's radar picked me up. He sniffed the air hungrily, sharpened his teeth, and started to drool. The beast needed fresh meat.

I went to bed that night with a rare sinus headache that accelerated into an earache so painful that I wept. It was excruciating. My cavalier attitude regarding my lack of health insurance crumbled as I contemplated how I would pay for the treatment of this obvious brain tumor.

I decided the earache was an act of God designed to get me health insurance. I asked about the full-time salary the next day. It was more than I had ever earned, and the CFO assured me I'd get a $20,000 Christmas bonus. (It's called "hazard pay.") Working there was commensurate with employment at a nuclear reactor facility. You never knew when Mr. Black was going to meltdown.

I trembled, feeling my mortal weakness. "Please, God. Give me the strength to make it to Christmas." I wanted that money. Would I be as ruthless as Mr. Black to get it?

Within hours of my signing a contract, Mr. Black was bellowing again. Sauron's eye was directly on me this time. I barely got through "the longest day"—day one of my full-time incarceration. My life flashing before my eyes, I bought five pairs of shoes to console myself about the pact I'd just signed with the devil. My face frozen, I gripped the shopping bags tightly as I walked home, fantasizing about life outside of Abu Ghraib's chic New York City outpost. What had I done?

Our first showdown occurred over the seemingly innocent topic of party invitations. Mr. Black was on every conceivable board of directors for hospitals, corporations, and museums. He wanted his name plastered everywhere to insure his immortality, at least as far as plaques and hospital wings were concerned. He received requests for money from all sorts of organizations. I vetted them. He donated to both political parties but I decided that he would not be donating to Bush on my watch. No matter how many pounds of paper I tossed in the recycling bin, there were still piles of invitations to attend to. I sat down at his desk with a calendar, the invites, and a pad and pen to strategize his social agenda. As invite after invite was addressed and dispensed with, the tension in the room grew. *Everything* irritated this man. Even festive party requests. I was distinctly uncomfortable being subjected to face time with Sauron.

He had several invites for one night. When I explained this and asked which he preferred, he became flustered and snapped, "What the hell are you talking about? You're trying to confuse me!"

I snapped right back. "I am *not* trying to confuse you. *And stop yelling at me!*" You could have heard a pin drop in the office outside. Everyone and everything froze, including the fax machine. All eyes and ears were affixed to the glass doors opening onto his office. And what do you think happened next? Would you expect the old man to break into a broad and sunny grin as if he'd just heard the best news of his life? Well, that's exactly what happened.

"Now, *that's* the spirit! You've got what it takes to *work* in this office! *You've got to fight back.*"

I was appalled. A man smiles with joy after being snapped at? Now he switched gears again and grinned sheepishly, even coyly. "Do you forgive me?"

He beamed like the Grinch. I remained utterly unmoved by this insane concoction of cruelty and contriteness. In fact, I now hated him even more. My stomach was twisting in knots. I mumbled "Yes" by way of apology without making the slightest effort to crack even a conciliatory smile. I dissembled with words, but not affect.

I realized how sick he was to enjoy this type of exchange—this venomous jousting. It gave him a cheap thrill. I decided that not only was he a sadist, but most assuredly he was a masochist, too. He *loved* it when I lashed out. It occurred to me then that he probably paid girls to whip and debase him after hours. The depths of the old geezer's depravity ran deep.

After he got his antagonism "high," I was even more skittish working there. Sure, everyone in the office regarded me as a rock star after our scrap, including the boss's grown son, the VP, CFO or something or other of one of his subsidiaries.

He never stood up to his daddy. In fact, he even married a *girl* to avoid the ire of his homophobic dad. But once this episode occurred, I knew Sauron would get hungry again, and need another adrenaline "fix." The tension built as we waited with baited breath for the other shoe to drop. It was only a matter of days.

One afternoon Jane told me to get Mr. Black some chocolate frozen yogurt. Mission impossible. This was 2006—well after the frozen yogurt boom of the '80s and well before Pinkberry exploded onto the scene, putting frozen yogurt virtually on every street in New York City. Our midtown deli carried salami and Gatorade.

I called with the results of my deli due diligence. "No yogurt. Only Haagen Dazs," hoping she would let it go.

She said, "Buy the Haagen Dazs and lie. Put it in a bowl."

My stomach sank.

Jane lied to Mr. Black all the time. It was her survival mechanism, and it worked. No one picked up his phone? "The phone lines were down." She had her hair done at lunch? "I was walking my dog."

I asked her, "What's your dog's name, Haagen Dazs?"

I bought the ice cream, released it from the paper cup, and buried the evidence deep in the trash. I nervously presented the frozen dessert to him in a china bowl with a silver spoon. The red eye of Sauron shifted slowly toward me. "What is this?" he inquired suspiciously.

Why was he questioning it? I mean, did it *look* like a cheeseburger? He asked for chocolate frozen yogurt. It was brown. It was frozen. It was in a bowl.

I didn't know how to respond. I hated lying, but I couldn't in this circumstance tell him the truth. "Columbo." I replied starkly.

"That's a brand! I asked you *what it is*," he glowered.

"I know it's a *brand*. It's *Columbo* brand!" I shot back. I swiftly ran through the current yogurt brands in my head, Stonyfield, Dannon (was Dannon even still around?) and prayed that Columbo was still in business since Mr. Black was a corporate brand maven.

He stared at me and I stared back in our Mexican ice cream standoff. The bowl remained clutched in my outstretched hand. He refused to take it. Very careful not to get the answer wrong and not wanting to lie further I submitted quietly, "It's chocolate."

"*Take this away*!!!" he exploded. "You're not answering my question! Why is it so hard to get a straight answer out of you?"

I pulled the offending bowl back and blurted, "It's chocolate yogurt!"

"Well why didn't you say that in the first place? What's wrong with you? Give me that!" He snatched the bowl and polished off the Haagen Dazs in seconds.

Thirty minutes later I was called into his office with Jane. She remained mute while he grilled me. "I don't understand why you can't give me a straight answer."

"Well, I assume—" I started.

He snapped, "*Never* assume anything."

I repeated firmly, "I *assume*—"

He stopped me again, "Never assume!"

How dare he ask me a question then censor me before I respond? I took a deep breath then exploded, "*I assume that if Jane tells me to get you something, it's because you asked for it and if I get for you, it's what you wanted*!"

He seemed at a loss and fumbled a bit. "Well, well, I am just *sick* of your excuses, and...and you're *twisting* everything around."

There was no winning with this man. I looked at him boldly, directly, and said quietly but bristling with bile, "You—Are—Perverse."

He stared at me, speechless. I stared back. He remained silent so I exited the room.

The old man left the office shortly after, had a panic attack that night, and ended up in the emergency room. It did not immediately occur to me that my three little words might have had something to do with his little excursion to the hospital. My weapon of mass destruction? The truth.

It took him 24 hours to decide he never wanted to see me again. Goodbye steady income, goodbye health insurance. I returned three of the five pairs of shoes I'd bought upon going full-time.

I was grateful that the brain tumor was gone and that I hadn't bought that chandelier in Soho last weekend. But my mission was accomplished.

I was free again. I went to yoga to work out the kinks. I left the twists to the pretzels in the office and the man who ate them.

CHAPTER 10

The Flood

My mother died the day before Mother's Day, many years ago. I didn't take it well. At 22 I thought I was old enough to be able to handle all that life handed me. After all, it was my karma. I was all grown up. Now I look at kids fresh out of college, see their baby faces, and understand exactly how much they don't know—their primary concern being what to wear and how to have fun. These concepts were alien to me—fun being the farthest thing from my mind. I was mature, old beyond my years, but still too tender to handle that tragic plot point, intensified by the fact that I'd already lost my father when I was five. Anything but bright eyed and bushy tailed, *no* part of me looked forward to the future. I was hundreds, no thousands of years old. I was the very essence of middle-aged. I look younger now than I did at 22. I had the weight of the world on my shoulders, and frankly, should have dated Atlas. Since my mother died, I have raised myself.

A Phi Beta Kappa graduate of The Misery Mystery School, I pulled myself up by my own bootstraps, something I encourage others to do. Suck it up. Deal with it. Of course, "dealing" can mean feeling like a baby, crying, journaling, sulking, skulking, processing, getting angry, healing, releasing, taking classes, getting therapy, and getting angry again. Dealing looks like different things to all of us, but there is always a process of digestion, of movement. A progression. If one takes action. Even if the action feels like one step forward, two steps back.

Life moves like a spiral. If you're worth even the tiniest bit of your salt, you are progressing upward, even if it feels like you're cycling through the same muck over and over. You are. It's your "issue." Confronting it again is how you overcome it. Consider that each time you cycle through a mud-zone, you are approaching the problem from a progressively higher and higher perspective, a graduate course, if you will, in overcoming your crap. Compare where you are to the larval stage you were in when you first confronted your old demon, your good enemy, the very challenge you chose to take on before birth in this lifetime. We're here to learn, to grow, and to expand the glory of God. Since We are God, and God is Love, we're ultimately here to learn how to be happier and shine like the sun. We are the light of the world. Because we live in a realm of light and shadow we must learn to navigate wisely. That is our job. It's like a computer game. Many mystic traditions say that life is literally, just that. We are navigating the course of this game to master our skills. The rewards are many and great. We are ready to start receiving them as the cosmic party is ushered in. Our gifts and pleasures will expand from here—this is just the start.

I've cycled and recycled my issues of love and loss, making great progress balancing myself and mastering my emotions. I believe I'm not only healing the pain of this lifetime, but the pain and misery of lives past, present (yes, we have parallel lives) and future. This is quantum stuff. My current lifetime's quota of grief extended above and beyond the call of duty. I'm not blaming circumstances. I'm simply describing how it felt to me. I was dumb struck, rendered lifeless, and hopeless. I am convinced that the perceived absence of love (I am referring exclusively to my parents, not the males I dabbled romantically with who offered shadows of love at best) echoes the howling wounds of lifetimes past. I am healing all lifetimes simultaneously, as if playing chess on a 3D platform. This pain goes deep. The healing deeper. I've drunk liquid Drano to plumb the depths and clear the path. My power and learning has grown commensurately.

Two and a half weeks ago I was pondering the meaning of multi-dimensionality and inter-dimensionality as I often do (the second most important thought after "What's for lunch?"). My head is filled with beautiful, inspirational thoughts, and this is why my life has become better. I almost exclusively read *The Sedona Journal of Emergence* an (almost) all channeled journal. I read tons of mystical books too, but no fiction. I find nonfiction strange enough. I don't watch TV. I rent inspirational or provocative documentaries, and yes, I like funny stuff too, though most current fare I find insipid. I've been exploring good old-timey cartoons like *Looney Tunes*, *Silly Symphonies*, *Betty Boop*, *The Little Rascals*, and *He's Your Dog, Charlie Brown*.

Anyhoo, as I got off my apartment building's elevator at night, a movie popped into my consciousness from out of nowhere. This is called a "psychic impression." When a thought has nothing directly to do with what you were musing about, it was implanted from your subconscious, from an angel, guardian, spirit, or teacher. The movie that came to me was *The Last Wave*, directed by

Peter Weir (1977) one of my Weir favorites along with *Picnic at Hanging Rock, Gallipoli, The Year of Living Dangerously* (when Mel Gibson was nothing but gorgeous, no crazy in sight), and *Witness*. Weir has a flair for the supernatural. *The Last Wave* is an apocalyptic, aboriginal, shamanistic, exploration of visions of the end of the world by water. Richard Chamberlain stars. I now present a timeline:

The following morning I pulled a tarot card from three different decks, as I do every day. One was "Trust," the next was "Ask Arch Angel Michael to Help You With This Situation" and the last was "Signs." I then bumped into a very sweet young neighbor. She lives with her boyfriend in a studio apartment. I've been friendly with them both for a few years, but had never invited her in until this day. I was inspired and showed her around. Since I have ample breathing room, I asked her how long she and her beau thought they would continue to live in their tiny abode. She said they planned to move to Connecticut in five, maybe ten years' time. I put myself on the line and suggested that they might want to skew their goal closer to five years rather than ten.

"With global warming and scientific and spiritual predictions backing it up, I believe New York will flood within five years. Water levels are supposed to go up two feet." Heck, lower Manhattan was evacuated with Hurricane Irene, which was practically a non-event (in Manhattan). And we now have Sandy under our belt, which most assuredly was an event. I don't fancy being evacuated from my island. Coastal folk everywhere be forewarned. Moving 200 feet above sea level is advised. Better safe than sorry, I plan to be the little piggy in the brick house. Somewhere else.

My neighbor left and I scooted over to my gym for a class. Afterward, for some reason I was "inspired" to drop in nearby shop CB2 and look at rugs. I didn't need rugs. But there they were, all pretty, and I wanted them. Oh well. Came home. Ate lunch. Got up and noticed water pouring into my hallway like blood gushing from a freshly shot body. I looked in my bedroom. It was filled with water. As in *filled*. There were two inches everywhere. I gasped.

My dog came over to investigate and since her legs are only 3 inches, was now paddling. The look on her face expressed, "Why am I swimming in my home?"

I quickly got help from the building staff and they were floored. One guy said he'd never seen anything like it. It was the worst flood he'd seen in this building. (I like to make an impression). A water line had exploded right by my bed (it handles the run off from the central air conditioning system. The pipes from 1960 were rusted through). Four workers in all (this does not include the superintendent and two plumbers who broke a cave sized hole in my wall to replace the pipes) rushed to remove 300 gallons of filthy water from my home. My apartment was inundated with murky (some of it was outright brown) liquid. So much for lunch.

Four men vacuumed and mopped the water. Electrical wires shorted and spurted on the floor. I scrambled to unplug things and pull cords out of the water. Had I not been home a fire would have broken out and my dog and cat would have been electrocuted. This started at 12:30 p.m. I had a 4 p.m. rehearsal and two performances that night at 7 and 9 p.m. of an abbreviated radio show version of Noel Coward's *Blithe Spirit*. I arrived at the theatre a little less polished looking and feeling than I would have liked. I was as blithe as I could be. But I was dry. Among my many personal effects ruined were my rugs.

When I went to the theatre at 4 p.m. I passed by the Columbus Circle fountain. It too was flooded, something

I'd never seen before. I jumped puddles and rivulets as I ran to catch my train. Later at the theater, I eyed one of the maintenance guys carrying a huge bucket of water. I wondered what he was doing with it. We broke shortly after for dinner. As I ascended the stairs to the street this same fellow tossed that very bucket of water right in front of my feet to clean the stairs. There was no mistaking it. This was a very watery day.

Three weeks later, to the day, I was walking home from the gym at lunchtime carrying an assortment of organic greens. Not thinking any particular thoughts, another "psychic impression" hit me. This time like a thud. I felt punched in the stomach. In all the years I never had this realization about the time period when my mother died. For all her over-protecting, stage-mothering, planning, and preparing me for everything from piano lessons, violin lessons, music camp, to competitive schools and programs, all the micro-managing came to a crashing halt when she became gravely ill for the last two years of her life. This put a pall on my last two years of college, and my life afterward in general. On the "bright" side, I wasn't filled with false hope. We both knew it was the end (she had pancreatic cancer and type II diabetes for years before that). Instead of planning for my life, we were planning for her death.

As much as she adored me (I don't question that for a second) I do not blame her for the implications of this realization that "came to me." She didn't discuss my future with me in any way, shape, or form other than advising me to rent out the master bedroom of our apartment to a businessman who would pay the rent and never be home. She was efficient. She kissed me goodbye and that was that, dying a month before I graduated college. No talk of my future, what I would do for work, did I want to have kids, what would I do that first year out of school.

Nothing. Nada. She was consumed with pain and she had work to do. She was dying.

I was left holding the keys to an apartment brimming with silence and darkest gloom. The realization that her motherly duties terminated on some level with her deadly diagnosis had never occurred to me. I knew I'd had it hard, but I thought that at 22, being well-educated and left with some security so I did not have to waitress or temp in order to pursue my artistic career, I had nothing to complain about, right? That's what other people seemed to think.

"You're so lucky!" they said when they saw my beautiful home.

Lucky. Yes. Right. Thank you. I mean, Fuck you. *Fuck* you. There was no one luckier than me. A nice apartment in New York City is reason enough to be grateful. For the shallow. I yearned for what was no longer there. Family was gone.

I believe my mother seeded this "psychic impression" about her lack of regard for my future. Sure, she'd said "You'll do fine" (a vague "plan" at best) and "You'll have a wonderful husband" (jury's still out on that one). The psychic impression my mother planted was a twofold gift. First, she was apologizing for neglecting to have discussions about my future with me. Second, I realized I deserved increased credit for handling that enormous challenge on top of working with her hospice nurse, organizing her cremation, taking tender care of her, handling her affairs, and being traumatized by her impending loss (all while going to school). I didn't feel sorry for my lot, I just felt really, really sad, and chided myself for not being happy and normal like other kids, for not dating and having sex and being cute and successful and married and birthing babies and settling down in a beautiful home or a Ralph Lauren ad.

On to the Lesson, the Bigger Gift, not of the psychic impression shared with me this week, but of this perceived "loss" of love in my life. First, it helped me to *perfect* my keening and wailing skills (I'm a comedian, people, laugh with me.). Additionally, the lack of external guidance forced me to turn within for my own answers. Hard, but important. And while I had been spiritual my whole life, this "lack" also turned me intensely toward the spirit world for both comfort and guidance. It was a perfect plan. Does my soul know how to design a curriculum, or what? If I'm not enlightened by the time I croak, I want my money back.

Tears started pouring down my face on the corner of this busy intersection as waves of understanding, no *waves of compassion for myself*, hit me. The floodgates opened and I cried the short walk home, clutching my organic greens. When I got upstairs, I cried some more. In some ways it felt like I was reliving her original loss those many years ago. The emotions and memories were close to the surface. I managed to choke down some lunch, dry my tears, then cried some more. (I'm a very thorough person). It occurred to me then that her death date, and the inevitable associated mother's day was right around the corner, five and seven days away, respectively.

When I went to the bathroom to wash my face, the sink backed up. What was this? One of the workers in my building had snaked my sink not three months ago. It was a big deal. I don't think in all the years I've lived in this apartment I've had the sink snaked. And it's backed up again? Now? After the flood? My sink bubbled up with filth, hair (not mine), and, gag, a cigarette butt (again, not mine).

I was nauseated, but took to cleaning and clearing the clog myself with pliers and a screwdriver. I pulled out the muck. I figured it was leftover from the flood when they dumped gallons of filthy water in my sink, my toilet, my tub, and my kitchen sink. So here I was, three weeks later, still clearing it up. Once I got over the disgust and had removed the detritus, it hit me again. I've been cleaning my pipes. Cleaning and clearing the pain, the dirt, the emotional detritus from my whole life, not just my mom's death, but my dad's as well, my loneliness, and the loneliness, grief, and abandonment of lifetimes untold. We've all suffered plenty here on Planet Earth. In fact, I believe as we clear our personal crap, we help uplift the energy of the entire planet. Score another one for The Light, not just a paltry thousand points, but *billions*. Your happiness means the world to The World. Prioritize it. Make it happen. We are all far more important than we think we are. Mother Earth and Father Sky are counting on us. That is what The Ascension is. Raise your Eyes up to the Heavens and your Heart to the Sky.

So here was this symbolic purge; yet more gunk cleared. I know a good sign (remember, I'd pulled the "signs" card?) when I see one. I was pleased. First, the flood washes me clean, then weeks later, deeper levels of gunk come up and out for my rebirth.

A postscript. While downtown yesterday, something caught my eye and glistened on a beautiful tree lined street, one of those old New York streets with brownstones, plants, flower boxes and iron gates. I was breathing in the day, the sun, the plants shiny from that morning's purifying rain. I looked at then smelled the flowers. Said a friendly "Hello" to them. They represent the elemental world. The world of plants and rocks are alive.

But what was this flashing thing that stopped me, and could I find it again? There it was. Like a diamond nestled in a fresh green plant, a brilliant light gleamed and shone. It beamed bright light at me like an unblinking strobe, first green, then orange, then yellow. If I shifted the tiniest bit it then shone red, violet, and blue. All the colors of the visible spectrum (I say visible because there are way more colors and sounds that we are not attuned to in this dimension). I stood there a full five minutes taking in the glory of this tiny *speck*. What was it? I concluded it was a drop of water that the sun was hitting in most perfect, miraculous fashion. Nowhere evident was its watery makeup. Only light and color were visible, scarcely bigger than a pinpoint (an eighth of a carat, shall we say?). But it was a gift. A promise. Of life, love, and hope. Perhaps that came from my mother, too. Perhaps it was from an angel, or from—it doesn't really matter. What matters is that it was there. And I saw it.

I believe my work is done. Not completely, 'cause then I'd be dead, which sounds great to me on days when I have to vacuum. This world is beautiful but lord, the dirt. I keep asking no one in particular when the maid is arriving and the answer is always, annoyingly, "When you hire one." For all my trouble, I now boast a deep wisdom and a profound immaturity (my euphemism for playful irreverence).

I've decided today is my graduation day, my true graduation of years and years of recovering from the darkest depths of despair. I did it. I'm proud of myself. I know my mom is proud of me, too. I just cracked open a bottle of prosecco to celebrate. This date represents my mother's release from excruciating pain and a brave life—her Independence Day. It is my Independence Day, too. I celebrate our freedom.

CHAPTER 11

Three Sisters

My wedding anniversary was earlier this month. Of course, that marriage ended many years ago, but the date was a landmark. "Many years" means something when you have a healthy, loving, supportive, and productive relationship. For me, it was just the passage of time.

Two buddies were meeting for a BBQ dinner that night and invited me extemporaneously. It was at one of the very restaurants that my ex and I dined at frequently. It was cheap, and it was fun. But I literally had not been there in years. I thought it a fabulous way to celebrate the date, with two true friends.

Right before meeting them I watched the bulk of *Project Nim*, a documentary about chimpanzee Nim Chimpsky (a play on Noam Chomsky, the brilliant American activist-philosopher). I wrote an essay on little Nim when I was in grade school, and how he was taught ASL (American Sign Language, or Ameslan). At college I became friends with a girl who studied with one of little Nim's trainers, another girl. Turns out most of Nim's trainers/caretakers were women, to one extent or another either lovers of the man who spearheaded the project, Herb Terrace of Columbia University, or under the spell of his dreams for the project. Little Nim was ripped from his mother's arms days after birth, a crime traumatic to both baby and mother, as it is with all animals stolen from their mothers for "experimentation", or our "entertainment."

Nim was passed from home to home and trainer to trainer, and finally, when Nim became too troublesome and dangerous (chimps are wild animals, after all, and very powerful) Terrace dumped him in a facility in Oklahoma. No more conversations with human friends. No more training. He'd never even met another chimp. He was unceremoniously abandoned. Nim was only good to Herb as long as his academic project lasted, and when the book was written, goodbye Nim. From there Nim was sold to a medical research lab on Long Island and was put in a tiny cage where he was subjected to heinous "scientific" experiments, one of the cruelest things we do to animals. I wish animals could turn the tables on their tormenters, *Planet of the Apes* style. Maybe then a couple of people would start to "get it." Vivisection, anyone?

In a rather irritable mood, I set out to meet my pals for dinner—something I was looking forward to—but somehow, my anger over the cruel treatment of Nim, my anger/frustration at the cruel treatment of billions of animals generally, was welling up in me.

When I met the boys they were having a grand old time at the bar, drinking Bull Dogs. Leave it to Americans to come up with *this* one: A "Texas" size frozen margarita with extra fruit flavor embedded with an upside-down, mini Corona beer, as if the bottle had crash landed into the drink. A shot of tequila in a plastic "Yankees" test tube was sunk into the mix. It was a battleship.

The sight of it made me laugh. My friends were laughing, too. But then, they were drinking it.

I abstained throughout dinner but finally agreed to split a Bull Dog with the boys for dessert. It was tasty, the beer cutting the sweetness of the frozen margarita. Still, what a Rube Goldberg of a drink. It reminded me of dessert at Serendipity. A fun joint filled with Tiffany lamps and an old-timey ice cream parlor atmosphere. Andy Warhol, Jackie O., and other sugar addicted luminaries have hung out there since the 1950s. Serendipity's gigundo banana split sports a whole banana jutting up at a pornographically suggestive angle (the restaurant is run by gay men—fabulous sense of humor in full display). Their hot fudge sundae spouts gloppy hot fudge like lava all over the dessert and its environs. It's extravagant.

But not as excessive as their "Cheesecake Vesuvius." No, *this* dessert goes too, too far. In fact it's indecent and should be arrested. An entire cheesecake (back in the day) was topped with a complete hot fudge sundae. Are you nauseated thinking about it? I was. It's like topping pizza with a bacon cheeseburger. And fries. My friends ordered Vesuvius and I took a bite. It was not disgusting. However, this kind of behavior should not be encouraged. It's Nero at the end of Rome kind of eating. I don't want to be carried out on a stretcher after a meal. Rather, not anymore.

When I was younger I used to eat 'til it hurt. Not all the time, but enough. After a friend and I had dinner at Serendipity (everything is oversized there) we ordered dessert. The trim gay waiter chided us. "One or the other, girls. Dinner *or* dessert. You cannot have both."

We paid him under the table and he brought our black market frozen hot chocolate and chocolate blackout cake. No stretcher, but plenty of pudge.

Back to the BBQ joint and my wedding "anniversary." Talk amongst the three of us turned to relationships. One of my friends is gay and had had one long-term live-in relationship. He described it as bad, not right, a waste of time that went on too long. I begged to differ. I believe all our choices are fabulous, unless, of course, you end up dead from them, but even then, I'm a karma/reincarnation gal. Your soul chose that experience for a reason. Life doesn't end after just one pesky death.

My marriage was difficult, but I don't regret it. I put up with a lot of shit I wouldn't contemplate for half a second today. But there were reasons I put up with it then, low self-esteem, a desire for family, a sense of belonging, and I did love the guy. He loved me too, just didn't waste much time or energy showing it. It was very sad for me to be with someone I loved who didn't give me the time of day. I know now he was a reflection for how I felt about myself. Not great. When you walk around with deep, dark energy, that's what you attract. Enter, my ex.

I dreamt recently that a famous director was reviewing a movie my ex was in (he's not an actor) and said, "The movie was terrible but his performance was great!"

I remember thinking "Ha!" in my dream, but when I woke up it made sense. My ex played exactly the role I hired him to perform. He was a kick in the pants, and one I sorely needed. Yes, it made me more sore, but if you're being attacked by a hornet's nest, you can't wallow in sadness, can you? You have to run for your life. By the time that relationship was over I was as mad as a hornet myself. You cannot be both depressed and angry simultaneously. One state is passive, the other active. Exit depression. Enter anger. It was progress.

I took that anger and ran with it, getting a job, a starring role in a musical, and, amusingly, slept again with the fellow I had lost my virginity to. When I bumped into him he said, "I heard you got married—"

"*Divorced*," I quickly corrected him.

Chemistry still in the air, we picked up where we left off. He was the first guy I slept with after my ex. It was a graduation of sorts. The boy I was hung up over years ago was now just a pleasant romp in the hay. Not only that, but I had the pleasure of approaching our rendezvous as a sexually seasoned woman, not a nervous ingénue. He apologized for not being able to stay the night.

"Who cares?" I thought, but said instead, "No problem."

I wasn't looking for "more" this time. I was merely flexing my sexual muscles. However, amused by the fact of his entering my sexual orbit a second time in seemingly random fashion I observed, "You know…you've unplugged me twice now."

Back to dinner. My friend David reminded me that at my "divorce party" I taped the divorce decree to my front door.

"Really?" I had *absolutely* no recollection of this, but it impressed the hell out of me.

What a fabulous idea. The decree was my Christmas wreath, my Easter Bunny, my ticket to freedom. I worked hard to get that divorce, wending my way through the New York Court House to get papers stamped, copied, and approved, a scary but satisfying accomplishment (we went for a low rent, "do it yourself" divorce, and yet again, the "do it" person in our relationship was me). I worked just as hard to create the wedding and the relationship. Love shouldn't be that hard. I ordered a divorce cake for my "coming out" party. I was torn between, "One Down And One To Go" and "Divorced And Available" for the decoration. I bought myself a "divorce ring."

My ex complained about my sweet tooth just as he had grumbled to company about the birthday cake I baked him ("I like pies," he groused). Now I was free to eat as much cake as I desired. If I wanted "Cheesecake Vesuvius" every goddamn day, I could have it (if I also wanted to look like Jabba the Hut). I used to get cakes from The Cupcake Cafe, a dumpy coffee shop in Hell's Kitchen, right by the even dumpier Port Authority Bus Terminal. In the midst of this tiny, tin-ceilinged truck stop one could purchase veritable masterpieces of flour, butter, and sugar. Each cake was topped with an explosive buttercream bouquet inspired by Renoir, Van Gogh, or Monet. They made small cakes and were so affordable (then) that I decided I didn't need a birthday or a divorce to indulge myself. I could just buy one to celebrate, oh, say, "Wednesday." There was no one there to criticize me anymore. I was free.

When my ex left (on Independence Day, no less) I was concerned that I would feel an abyss of despair as I did when my mother died. I was in an apartment brimming with silence. I awaited devastation. Nothing happened. Then it dawned on me. My new life dawned on me. *This* silence was an *absence* from pain. No more irritation. No more heartbreak. My home was a sanctuary. The demise of the relationship transformed a mortuary into a refuge. These days, it's even a bit of a ballroom and concert hall. I celebrate breakfast, lunch, dinner, and my ability to nap, unencumbered. I celebrate my freedom to write, act, and exercise. To be alone. Or not. My life is full of Me.

The day after the BBQ dinner was gray, rainy, and cold and I awoke with a tinge of sadness. Why? Was I too flippant about being relieved about the demise of my marriage? My normal Thursday routine was to head downtown to take my favorite sculpt class at the gym, but

I just wasn't feeling it. I hadn't been to the gym in a week. Was I sliding backward? The self-recriminating began. Of course, I was still sore from a brutal Tui-Na massage a few days prior, a pressure point "Raid at Entebbe" on my body. During the "massage" I called out to Jesus, Mother Mary, and eventually Quan Yin since the modality was Chinese. My muscles were super tight from exercising. I swore never to exercise again.

I prayed for guidance from Spirit to "help me feel better," honored my desire to stay home, and took my dog for a walk. Normally I head east to do so, but today I was inspired to go west. Within a few yards I saw three blonde women looking my way and smiling at my dog's goofy walk/hop. She's a natural comedian and lover of most people and dogs. She's been my happiness coach for the last four years. If I look a little down, she catches my eye with her soft brown ones, wags her tail, and says, "What's for lunch?"

There's not much a walk in the fresh air with a good friend can't help.

The Three Muses smiled brighter as we approached and were thrilled when we stopped to engage with them. My dog said hello and kissed them. They cooed and lit up. I asked them what they were waiting for under the trees of my very verdant block.

"The Jitney," they said.

Ah, the Hampton Jitney, a luxury bus taking them to a long luxury weekend. How nice, I thought. They must have a home there, and even though it was a glum day, getting away to a fireplace and a vacation home, well, that's just swell.

"The Hampton Jitney?" I asked.

"No," one corrected me. "Sloan Kettering."

"Oh," I gulped. There could be no greater disparity between the two. Sloan Kettering is a cancer hospital. My home is sandwiched between their two treatment outposts. In the past, their entrance was surrounded by scrubbed workers on break puffing furiously on their cigarettes. It's probably a "no smoking zone" now, as most of New York City is (including parks).

"Who has cancer?" I asked as I looked at the three.

"I do," said the one in the middle. She was a beautiful blonde girl who claimed 41 years but looked 31 tops. To her right was her lovely petite blonde mum, complete with English accent. She was a cozy woman, warm, calm, and loving. To her left was her American gal-pal, a fellow flight attendant at United (newly merged with Continental, "Bad merger" they both said as they shook their heads). American gal-pal was a tall, skinny drink of water with TV "Flo's" sass and brass. She was tanned and wrinkled to within an inch of her life. Her demeanor and look screamed Texas to me, but she was from Colorado, an American Classic, a female version of actor Scott Glenn. I liked her immediately. I liked them all.

The girl with cancer looked pregnant. It was in her stomach. She was pregnant with cancer (or with anger, as I look at it). Louise Hay was one of the first to make the connection between disease and our emotions and thought patterns, and I'm with her all the way. Check out her classic book, *You Can Heal Your Life*. And before you get upset, it's not about blaming the patient. It's about empowering the patient to look at unhealthy patterns so that she can turn them around.

The girl was a gentle sweet thing with big, beautiful, earnest blue eyes. She had married an asshole of her own, a dashing (I imagine) Brit who worked for Cantor Fitzgerald at World Trade and managed *not* to get killed that day.

"Only the good die young," I muttered.

Apparently he was a cocky, no-good so-and-so. As with my own benign uterine fibroid tumors, Louise believes they tend to represent resentment, usually toward a partner. I can own that. I'm healing and releasing them naturally with acupuncture, vitamins, visualization, Chinese herbs, and good old-fashioned spiritual growth.

The girl gave her tumor a guy's name and said she was "getting rid of him." The thought of fighting cancer has always given me pause. It's in your body, so you're fighting something in you, fighting yourself, in a way. My mom had cancer so I'm an old pro at all the visualization techniques to "battle" the demon, starting in the 1970s with Dr. Bernie Siegel's work. I always thought transforming and releasing cancer via love was more appealing, but that's just me. I told the girl that since I created my fibroids with my thoughts and feelings I decided to view them as Centurions or Guards, safekeeping my precious uterus, person, creativity, and sexuality (that's the second, Sacral Chakra, color orange, representing creativity and sexuality) until the right, kind, gentle caring man came along to honor me and my Sacred Femininity. Instead of viewing them as alien and unwanted, I saw their unconscious creation as a sort of "hiring them for the job." They were not scabs. I contracted them to protect me until I felt safe again.

As I take my Chinese herbs I visualize the fibroids softening, releasing, and falling away in particles, naturally, like snow blowing off of a statue or rain gently falling. No more hardness. No more anger. No more defensiveness and fighting. A gentle releasing of the past, my pain, defensiveness, and hurt. I didn't want my castle vigilantly guarded anymore. I wanted peace to welcome a prince.

We talked about all this for a good half hour. They kept looking at their watches because the Jitney was due every ten minutes, yet persisted in not appearing. Their appointment was in half an hour. It was obvious to me that the bus was late because they were meant to talk about magic and healing with me and be loved, healed, and licked by my magic dog. No accidents.

As I walked away from them I realized that's why I wasn't at the gym that day. Clear as daylight. I had prayed to feel better and now I did. It often comes by connecting with others in love and light. As I help others to heal, laugh, feel, and think, I as surely am healed. As we teach, we learn. As we love, we are loved.

I dipped down again later that afternoon (yay, me!) feeling restless and anxious. I started to feel guilty, and to blame myself for sinking. I believe I create my moods, feelings, thoughts, and life. But blaming is totally different from taking responsibility. I have the power to do something about my moods, to understand and to transmute them. Sometimes a trip to the gym can help burn off that energy, just like a dog needs exercise. Sometimes a glass of wine and a snack or meal will do the trick. Sometimes a nap. Then I wonder, did the blackness even come from me? Is it free-floating anxiety from the ethers? Some of us are more sensitive to this than others, especially with all the negative planetary energy being cleared and released today. There are many possible explanations. The most important thing is that I explore different scenarios to love myself out of it, even if it means indulging my sadness, anger, or depression.

At a loss as to what to do, I returned a hat to a store. You would not believe the drama that went into this decision. I had just bought another, similar hat from the same store. Did I need both? Of course not. Did I have many other hats? You betcha. Do I look FABULOUS in all of them? Uh huh. Since I was feeling overwhelmed by THINGS lying around my house, I shoved the khaki

(What kind of a color is that for spring? Oh, but it looks cute on me, and maybe I could...) I SHOVED the hat in the bag, no looking back, except at my little pooch who begs to go EVERYWHERE with me, but NO, I must go, I must DO this thing. I open the door and who's in the hallway but my neighbor, Michelle, who just loves my dog and she lights up at the sight of her. Except it's not my neighbor. It's her identical twin.

I've met her before, this twin, but there's always the confusion if I see her alone without my neighbor and her boyfriend. Amusingly, just weeks ago, I invited my neighbor into my apartment for the first time. (see Chapter Eight, "The Flood"). We've been cordial for two years but recently, our lives have become more entwined.

My dog rushes out and starts to play in the hallway. My neighbor opens her door to receive her twin and the way becomes clear. I said, "You want my dog for an hour?"

"Yes!" the girls blurted together.

Everything was starting to flow now. People, smiles, dogs, wags, energy. The girls took my dog and I took a head-clearing walk and returned the offending hat. Sometimes the tiniest decision can have the most monumental effects. Nothing changes until something moves.

That evening my neighbor and her twin came over. We talked, cracked open some wine, and talked some more while sitting on the floor. The twin, too, had an asshole of note in her past. We indulged in girl talk. This day was full of healing and connecting with yet more people. Eventually my neighbor's beau came and joined us. A gentle soul, he is a model of the New Man. A classic, virile, Italian American, he is also gentle and quiet. He inevitably does the laundry when I do, and he grocery shops, too. He is all man but not macho, a hard worker, and a good partner. My neighbor's twin told me that he is as wonderful as he seems. One of those strong, silent types. However, when someone in their family (I'm guessing it was a bad boyfriend) needed putting in his place, she said Frank "did what he had to do." (I'm fantasizing it was a good right hook). There's nothing like a well-placed right hook when a thug is way out of line.

Just like the "street justice" my uncle Pete told me about from the 1920s and '30s. My mom and her brother grew up on the very street I live on now, about twenty yards west. The neighborhood was Italian, Greek, and Jewish. The kids played stickball, handball, jacks, marbles, and jumped rope outside. They owned the streets, and if a car dared trespass on their property, the kids slapped the car as it passed by and yelled at it to get off "their street." When my mom got hungry she shouted up to her window, "Ma!" Her mother lowered a basket on a rope with buttered, sugared bread.

One day a neighborhood girl got raped, and when the guys in the 'hood found out who did it, they threw him off a roof. Oh well! He should have thought about wanting to live before he raped the girl. There's something satisfying about that street justice to me. Yes, I'm all about love and light, but there's karma, too. This was no muss, no fuss, no messy trial, just a simple over the rails, "See ya!" She was "their girl," and it was "their neighborhood." Ah, the good old days.

My neighbors stayed for over four and a half hours. Time flew. Dinner was forgotten. A fellowship was forged, just like the one forged earlier on the street with three strangers, three sisters. I went to bed happy and full. Be gentle with yourself as you wend your way through the wilderness of your feelings and dreams. "Not all those who wander are lost." – J.R.R. Tolkien.

CHAPTER 12

Forgive Me Not

I rented a documentary on forgiveness. It was an hour-fifteen, something I thought would be uplifting and soothing on a cold and stormy June night (all bets are off with global warming weather. New York City shifts radically every ten minutes). Instead, I found myself bored and irritated. Which led me to ask several questions, because this film addressed none of them 1) what *is* forgiveness? 2) *why* should we forgive? 3) why is forgiveness so *hard*? 4) and, most important, *how* do we forgive? In other words, what are the *mechanics* of forgiving?

The movie started out well enough. Marianne Williamson was a featured speaker. She's very eloquent and charismatic though I find her books dull. Thomas More spoke. Snooze. Thich Nat Hahn yakked. Yawn. Don't get me started on Eckhart Tolle (he wasn't featured in the film, but just looking at him puts me in a coma). I love spirituality but does it always have to be so *boring*?

To for-give, for-go, let go of anger, hate, resentment, and judgment. Easier said than done, right? Just *let* it go?

Hell no. You better have some brilliant reasons why first. But we really need to understand the nature of "not forgiving," (or holding a grudge) before going further. We need *reasons* to reach *resolution*.

Believe it or not, there *are* very good reasons why we hold a grudge. When we withhold forgiveness we are expressing disapproval, disdain, or dismay regarding a person and/or their behavior. We hold that wall of judgment as our shield against them. "If I hate it enough, I'll make sure it never happens to me again."

We become like dogs, snarling at an enemy. However, this grudge can go on indefinitely, and then you are no longer fighting "what is." You are now fighting "what was."

The key thing to consider is that we are always doing the best we can to take care of ourselves based on our beliefs at the time. We never do anything without a reason. No matter how mixed up some of our logic may seem, the best of intentions lie beneath our actions, including holding a grudge. By examining *why* we do things, we can determine if our behavior is really as effective as we mean it to be.

Underlying our judgment is the belief that being angry is good, important, and useful. It defines our position. "Abortion is bad!" "Gay marriage is bad!" "Republicans are bad!" Our outrage defines who we are. A lot of people define who they are by what they hate. Gotta be a better way, dontcha think? Abhorring injustice doesn't fix a thing.

If we *didn't* proclaim our disapproval by hating something, what would *that* mean? Would it mean that we had no notion that a loved one being hurt was something we *didn't* want, and if we didn't care when it did happen, could it mean that in some way we actually *wanted* it? Just because you accept what happened doesn't mean you invited it. Forgiveness does not mean being stupid or without discernment. It does not mean wanting more "bad" people to do more "bad" things to you.

It means accepting that things do happen to us in life that we don't want, from losing a job to losing a loved one to breaking a nail or getting a splinter. When we get mad at these events, it's as if we lodge a complaint against the cosmos, as if railing at God or even the pain will prevent those things from happening again. Clearly, this does not work. Outrage does not stop the possibility of ever losing, being disappointed, grievously offended, or hurt again. Life dips and swells on an ongoing basis. Does raging at circumstance change a thing? I'll tell you what it does. It makes us more likely to go and stub our toe on top of everything else.

Now if I didn't express my disapproval toward the "bad" thing you did, then you would do it again, right? You would think I didn't care. That it didn't matter. What people need to consider is that there are many ways to protect ourselves that do not include holding constant angry vigils (an exhausting behavior to be sure). Believe it or not, emotions are behaviors. A behavior is something demonstrable. Sadness produces tears. Anger and happiness both change body chemistry.

Quite simply, we deem not forgiving to be useful. The unspoken rationale is that by hating what we don't want, we keep it at bay, like two north pole magnets eternally repelling each other. In holding an angry grudge (like fueling a fiery moat), we believe we can keep the "bad" (another way of simply saying "what we don't want,") away from us. If we decide the offending act was okay, then we wouldn't be looking out for our interests, right? If we thought it was *okay*, we would just invite that old murderer over for dinner and *laugh and laugh* like old war buddies and then what would he do? He'd up and murder *another* person during dinner. Murder me once, shame on you. Murder me twice, shame on me!

I'm not saying that if something "terrible" happens to you, that you are not entitled to your grief, sadness, irritation, confusion, anxiety, depression, or rage. You are entitled to react in any way you wish for as long you wish. However, to maintain an indefinite stance of judgment and disapproval (the opposite of forgiveness) has a high cost. It exacts a price on one's mental, emotional, spiritual, and physical health. You *can* resolve your emotional angst surrounding the event and still choose never to see the motherfucker who pissed you off ever again. You can be at peace with them and what they did (on some level) at a safe, safe distance. You do not have to remain friends, pretend that you like them, or hang with them again. See? That's what I was saying about learning to take care of and protect yourself (i.e., do your best to make sure it never happens again) without gnashing your teeth for the rest of your life (requiring a new set of choppers). For those who go deep in their forgiving and embrace the perpetrator, the level of healing goes quantum. This isn't a goal for everyone, but for those who go there…it's Jesus Land (don't be offended if you're not a JC fan, just substitute your favorite Action Hero).

Now let's utilize the rational mind to separate the "crime" from the person who committed it (we want to examine things from lots of angles). Can you do that? Go a step farther and look at your reaction to the event (screaming, thrashing, and cursing). Did you want the event to happen? Hell, no. Do you want it to happen again? Hell, no. Will your being pissed about it indefinitely prevent it from happening again or change the past? Not a chance.

Here's my magic key which enables one to downshift from full throttle rage into neutral, with the potential of someday going into total-forgiveness-reverse: I substitute the word *acceptance* for *forgiveness*. Forgiving seems to imply you condone or even approve of the event on some level, doesn't it? So, uh, let's say you killed someone I love. "I forgive you" has the implication (to me, and I suspect many others) of saying, "Gee, it's all right, it's not so bad, not so important, *don't worry about it.*" It seems to diminish the impact of the offence, right?

Forgiveness is not about diminishing or negating what was done. Nor is it about being "big" about it while looking down patronizingly in judgment. That's for "show." True forgiveness has nothing to do with show. If genuine humility and compassion is not involved, the point is missed. When true forgiveness happens, a merging of souls occurs between the aggrieved and the perpetrator. And in a way, the event disappears on some level. It doesn't mean that reparations are not owed or that punitive action is not demanded. It doesn't mean that you forget the whole thing. It means in some way the event has lost its emotional charge. The event is transformed. Sometimes even into something profound.

Romeo and Juliet offers a tragedy of endless grudges and vendettas that lead to endless bloodshed and killing. The futility of "an eye for an eye" mentality is made patently clear when everyone in the play (well, all the cute ones, anyway) ends up stone cold dead. Are the Capulets and Montagues happy? Nah, they're all fucking miserable. Vengeance is an exercise in futility. It neither removes your pain nor returns your dead to life. You're left right where you started, surrounded by yet more bloody mess and mayhem.

By the law of attraction (which I swear by, as with the law of gravity) the more focused we are on what disgusts, disturbs, and offends us, guess what we attract more of? Don't you know people who are ALWAYS complaining? Whine, whine, whine. The weather (too hot, too cold, too wet, can't win). Some people are always outraged, always offended, while others take or see little to no offense (Some, frankly, should take more. These are the people who set no boundaries whatsoever and let themselves be trampled upon). If you believe the world is full of sheisters and you have to be careful, you will attract sheisters and will have to be careful. We see what we want to see. The whiners inevitably have something to whine about. (I'm wending and winding my way around the issues. Sneaky, like).

Keep in mind when we learn to suck stuff up (it's up to you what, how deep, and when you suck) that there are profound lessons we just might be learning from these uncomfortable situations. Just as a child must learn to share toys and to control temper tantrums and that he does not get everything he wants whenever he wants it, we, too, as adults, must learn to accept that things come and go. Jobs. Marriages. Lives. Savings. Homes. This world is ephemeral and ain't called Maya (illusion) by the Hindus for nuttin'. We grasp at security where none exists. The only true serenity is the rock of faith and peace within us. Once we connect with that Source Energy, our circuits light up and we radiate like a Christmas tree.

Let me counter this by saying that "putting up with stuff" is not an invitation to let people walk all over you. Only Gandhi and Jesus did that really well, and they're in their own category. No, you and I, *we have to set boundaries*. Forgiving rudeness, neediness and other people's emotional parasitism, *not what I'm talking about*. That's another article altogether. Forgiving does not mean being a patsy or a pussy. If we ignore infractions like these, we invite them. We also encourage the offenders to keep on offending. It is important to speak uncomfortable truths, but know that this can be done comfortably. It's a learned skill. An art, really.

Get a lock for your door. Don't answer the phone when you don't want to talk. Listen to your feelings (they're an internal alarm system). If someone is perpetually pissing you off, it could be because you are perpetually *letting* them do what they want in your life instead of YOU doing what you want in your life. In which case you're really mad at yourself for being a big fat sucker, though you blame "them" instead. It's not them. It's you. Build some backbone. Just say no. *You* set the guidelines by which everyone treats you. They mimic how you behave. Take *care* of yourself. When you do, others will. The world reflects back how we feel about ourselves.

At root for most of us in our lack of forgiveness of others is our lack of compassion toward ourselves. As we see ourselves, so we see the world. If we are cold, hard, and unforgiving toward others…you fill in the blanks. If you have some huge, hardened rift in your life regarding another person or persons, look for where are you being judgmental and unforgiving toward yourself. Oops, there it is!

The next question is where has your lack of forgiveness and harsh, punitive sentence (guilt, self-hatred, low self-esteem) imposed by you, on you, gotten you? To walk around with negative self-judgment is akin to wearing a constant hair shirt. Does punishment really help? No, it exhausts, debilitates, (and chafes). Now, rehabilitation is a totally different concept. Just watch *The Dog Whisperer*. If you want to fix behavior, you have to *understand* behavior. Does punishment alone work to change a person? Of course not. We know that most imprisoned criminals come out of jail new and improved criminals. For there to be redemption there must be a softening of the heart and a widening of the mind. There must also be a *belief* that one *can* change, that one *can* be better, happier, free, and unencumbered. With this expansion of heart and mind comes the freedom for them both to work together and create miracles of healing.

When we view the world with a cynical and judgmental eye, it is inevitable that we view ourselves in the same light. Our ability to love and accept the world is as important as our ability to love ourselves "as is," human foibles and all (they're often what make us cute). Actually, our ability to love and forgive ourselves comes first and foremost. It starts with you. You cannot give to another what you do not give to yourself. Unconditional love starts at home.

Now, to espouse that one *should* forgive, or even that it is *good* to forgive, begs the issue of *why*. I believe in selfishness. I'm not talking about creepy, narcissistic selfishness, I'm talkin' about good, healthy self-love. Obviously, we define that in different ways, from sleeping in, eating chocolate, or quitting the job or marriage that just doesn't fit anymore. I do not believe in denying yourself, privation, or putting others before you. On the other hand, when you start to see that the other *is* you, when you do for others, you truly do receive gifts. It's "tricksy," like Gollum said.

You must balance your needs with the wants of others in your life. It's sort of a seesaw effect. A little love for me, a little love for you. Then there's the snowball-effect and the ever-popular "healing stampede" when the floodgates open. Love, forgiveness, and peace are sweet havens. It is SO much easier to love than to not love. Don't you feel *great* when you are loving? We are happy when we are loving and loving when we are happy. Love is our *essence*. God is joy. When we're not living from that place then we are swimming against the tide, going against the grain of Who We Really Are. When we do live from that place, being kind, considerate, loving, generous, and forgiving is as easy as breathing on a clear spring day. (If you have allergies, kindly pick an analogy which will not make you sneeze.)

Perpetually angry people inevitably have high blood pressure. I dated a guy who blamed his high blood pressure on me. He had it before dating me, and I'm confident he still has it. He found excuses for his anger everywhere, but never did bother to look in the mirror.

I believe there is a powerful connection between anger and cancer. Author and New Age guru Louise Hay pointed it out in her seminal book *You Can Heal Your Life*. Having seen firsthand the effects of anger on my mother's health, I can attest to the truth of this. She had a lot of unresolved anger as a relatively young widow. Because I *understand* why, I totally forgive her for the times she took it out on me. Anger eats at you, literally and figuratively. She died a long, slow, painful cancer death. She didn't have the means then to work out her shit the way I do now, with New Age teachings gushing all over the place. Also, she never drank or dated, and frankly, it would have loosened her up. She was tightly wound with only tennis for release. Tennis just goes so far. We have to heal ourselves physically, emotionally, mentally, and spiritually. No facet can be ignored.

Now, does everyone who gets cancer have anger as its primary genesis? How would I know? Louise's diagnoses of attitudinal causes are generalizations, but I've found her long list of diseases and "causal" thought patterns to be dead on. Certainly they are for me and my "issues." I've got a mirror. I use it.

Because anger is toxic, a grudge (no matter how small) is a ticking time bomb for the grudge bearer. Anger is slow death. But you can't "just" forgive someone, even for your health. You have to have *reason* to forgive beyond "you should." You can't force it. And here's the catch I don't think most folks talk about—it helps to try to understand the offender. When all you look at is your being offended (let's take the extreme case of having someone you love murdered) you probably have no understanding, (nor desire) to understand the offender. They're just "Bad." "Evil." "Terrible." "Terrorists." "Devils." I think turning the other cheek means contemplating what motivates the other guy. Now, when you're hurting, do you necessarily give a shit? Probably not. But if you want to crawl out of the snake pit of despair you are writhing in, if you want to heal and move on with your life and not develop an ulcer or worse, then it behooves you to contemplate the big picture. Even if you are able to come to some understanding of why the "bad" guy did the "bad" thing, I still always say, "It's not an excuse. But it is an explanation."

    Let me give a pedestrian example of what I am talking about. There's a grumpy guy in my neighborhood who walks his snarly dog. I don't like either of them. First and foremost, my job is to protect my dog, who is sweet, submissive, and small. There are lots of folks in my neighborhood who claim their dogs are friendly right before they lunge for my little darling, who practically jumps into my arms with fright. The owner laughs off the aggression with a cackle. "Oh, she's just *playing*." Yes, and Al Capone was just flexing his trigger finger. I am not "forgiving" of these people. I'm not here to make friends with them or their fanged alter egos. I cross the street. Because my behavior speaks for itself, there is no need for me to hold a grudge. I don't have to hate them. I do have to take action. I avoid people with trigger-happy personalities where previously, I used to date them. Lesson learned.

I was with my pooch, the grumpy guy with aggressive dog, and another local with her annoying (to me) dog in our park. No, I do not love everybody equally. This does not mean I don't treat them with consideration. But I don't "pretend." You can be decent without laying on the BS. Both of their dogs steal my dog's ball, so I have to grab it quickly when I see either of them approach. After grumpy guy left, the lady turned to me confidentially. "You know, when I came here yesterday I found him crying."

That gave me pause. "Do you know why?" I inquired.

"He said his wife of 25 years died of cancer four months ago. They got the dog together when they found out she was terminal."

Oh. Did I feel differently about him when I learned this information? You betcha. Did I feel guilty for not liking him? Nope. Did I reach out, express my condolences, and try to talk to him the next time I saw him? Yup. Did we establish a heart-warming bond? Nope. He's still grumpy (or awkward) and also kinda deaf. Did he proceed to give my dog a treat *again* after I'd specifically asked him *not to* give her treats just the day before? Yup. Did his dog then steal the other lady's dog's toy? Yup. Was I relieved when they all left the park? You betcha.

But do you see my point? I'm not looking to be close to this man or his highwayman of a canine. But I do feel compassion for him and I am grateful for this new insight into his life. My perspective has softened.

Beyond Belief is a documentary about three 9/11 widows who decide to do something radical with their grief. Instead of just feeling sorry for themselves, they reach out to other grieving widows. In *Afghanistan*. Afghanistan has been war torn for decades now (I'm no expert, Wikipedia says since 1978). Yes, it sucked being a 9/11 widow. These women were grief-stricken wives and mothers. But instead of staying mired in *their* pain, they risked life and limb to connect with *others* in an impoverished and war torn country. The Afghani women were overwhelmingly warm and loving toward the Americans. They asked to see photos of their American homes. One of the Americans broke down crying and told her she couldn't, she was too embarrassed, for compared to the Afghani widows, the Americans lived like Saudi Royalty. The Americans decided to help the grieving Afghanis. They founded non-profit "Beyond the 11th" to help women who not only no longer have husbands, but have lost children to violence or starvation. These women have no rights and lack the barest of necessities. I mean they eat dirt for breakfast. The Americans transformed their grief and loss into compassion and generosity. Now *that* is alchemy.

We are all part of a whole. The beach doesn't exist without the gazillions of grains of sand that make up the shore. You can bask in your singularity or you can take a step back, or up, and look at the big picture. I believe in life after death and reincarnation. We are here to garner experience. We are here to *become* the experience, for you don't learn about a topic just by reading about it, do you? We've all "been there and done that" in the most extreme sense. We've been raped, murdered, and maligned. It gets even better when you consider that you've also raped, murdered, and maligned in past lives. That's where karma comes in. It's not punishment. It's learning through experience what it's like to be on both sides of a situation. We're here on Earth to receive a *rounded* education. Death just signals "Game Over" for this round. The pinball machine is reset. We start again (and yes, there's a rest, learning, and assessment period in between which is apparently *quite* delightful).

Now, does that help you when you're hurting (or hurling)? Nope. But we have the mental ability to come in and out of focus and oscillate between the big and the small pictures, the personal and the impersonal. Consider when someone "hurts" you that on a soul level, they are helping you to learn a lesson, as you are helping them to learn theirs. One hand washes the other. We are not one better than the other. Despite how enticingly easy it is to fall into that trap. How many people indignantly say "*Well*! I would *never* do that!"

How do you know, Miss Smarty-Pants? How do you know? You may be all smug and moral this life, but you may have been the biggest lying-thieving-murdering-slut in your last. Try to move into observer mode. With this bold step we transcend the dance of duality (push, pull, shove, drama, good, bad, right, wrong, yes, no, conflict, confrontation), out of polarity and right up into "triality," to the top of the pyramid, above the fray, spiritually speaking. Contemplate it. We're talking box seats at the game instead of wrestling in a mud pit. This is what's meant by being in this world but not of it.

One of the Ramtha books (channeled by J.Z. Knight) in the 1980s, asserts that nothing happens without our soul's approval (your soul is most definitely not your ego, which just wants ice cream, candy, foot rubs, and praise all day). I knew about *that* one. But when he stated that on a soul level there is a CONTRACT between a murder victim and a murderer, well, that just blew my mind. A wink, a nod, and a *handshake*? Are you KIDDING me? Unbelievable, but also very cool. If truly there is no death, as most of us believe, then one measly murder ain't gonna kill you (ha!). Your soul chose the experience as a karmic balancing since you killed someone in a past life, you lousy bum. Sure, being killed is annoying and scary and just might hurt, but how is it any different from having a horrific nightmare from which you wake up? Is it different from seeing *Texas Chainsaw Massacre*? (Why anyone watches horror movies is beyond me.) When you contemplate all the bloodbaths this planet has had, *is still having*, if you believe in reincarnation, you have to say the odds are pretty good you've been murdered, frozen, starved, strangled...yes! Fun for the whole family! Yet here we are again. We've lived to tell, and just like the kids' toy from the '70s ("Weebles wobble but they don't fall down") we're baaaaccckkk. So suck up your karma and stop whining. Life ain't for sissies. You don't want to have to come back next time and start from square one, do you? Learn those lessons! I did mention I was going to explore forgiveness from lots of angles. You were warned.

The forgiveness documentary also featured the Lancaster, Pennsylvania Amish whose young daughters were murdered or maimed at school by a man who then killed himself, leaving behind a wife and children. The Amish reached out to the murderer's family right away. Crikey. That's huge, but they did it all right. Went right over there. Comforted his wife, parents, and kids (this guy was obviously husband and father of the year, right?). Turns out he was a kiddie-diddler, too, so yes, the family he left behind could use TLC. That is some Big Amish Love.

The deepest rift in the forgiveness documentary seemed to generate from the trauma of 9/11. The "terrorists" were an obvious focal point for people's anger. Or, perhaps our government, which allowed it to happen? You don't need crazy conspiracy theorists to lay this one out for you. Check out the Architects and Engineers (not exactly the loopiest demographic) who have come forward to prove it in no way happened like the official story (Architects and Engineers AE911 Truth Action (ae911truth.org). Rent *Zeitgeist* and *Thrive* (or view them online for free). *In Plane Site* is another good documentary on the topic. If you're convinced that the official story is total bullshit, as I am, *then* whom do you get mad at? The man behind the man behind the man with the mask? How do you forgive someone and something you cannot even comprehend? You don't. You heal by *accepting* that which you cannot change. No use railing at a tornado. Get humble and *run*.

A 9/11 fireman's mom was featured. She was furious with the terrorists. At first. Then she was furious with *our* government for burying the pulverized ash (which obviously included human remains) in a garbage dump on Staten Island. Then I formed my own conclusion about whom she was really mad at. Herself. Her son, divorced with three kids, got remarried. She refused to attend the wedding and her son told her, "I'll never talk to you again."

They did talk again, but it was strained ever after and then he was killed. She was left with an oversize pile of regret. Regret's right up there with guilt and grudges. Ouch. This grieving mom found it easier to just stay mad at other people. If her son was alive, she'd still probably be bearing that old grudge against him for remarrying.

Suppressing emotion is not the answer, nor is anger a long-term stratagem. You'll end up like Al Pacino in *Carlito's Way*. Being angry all the time is like carrying an entire undigested pepperoni pizza around in your gut—it'll fester and you'll turn green. Accepting your emotions and assessing your beliefs will help to redeem you.

When you're reeling with rage, writhing with indignation, and railing at injustice, consider taking a step back. (I also recommend a good cry, a nap with your teddy bear, soup, and a glass of wine). It might take you months, maybe years to get to that "place of possibility." It could also take a minute. Consider that, by being compassionate with yourself, accepting (not condoning) what is, accepting what you cannot change, and humbly embracing your life's path (no matter how twisted and torn it may seem) it becomes possible to look at your "enemy" with compassionate eyes. "Forgive me" for saying this, but you just might find yourself looking in the mirror. Look with love.

CHAPTER 13

Candy-Assed Dating

I've endeavored to meet men in various, amusing ways. Case in point, I attended an event, which, unbeknownst to me, was exclusively gay. Fine, call me stupid. It all started innocently enough when I had my hair cut by a gay hairdresser in the Village, the West Village (gay speak for you non-New Yorkers). Are there straight people in the village? Absolutely, my parents were two of them in the 1950s when they first got married. They lived on Washington Place. The Village was and is an artistic enclave, and where artists lurk, there be gay folk.

I got a decent cut and liked my hairdresser. When we were talking he learned I was single and he invited me to the salon's Christmas party that very evening. It was an upscale joint, decorated with beautiful flowers and track lighting (I love bright, colorful lights. If there's a definition of hell for me it's bleak decor and fluorescent lighting). My hairdresser *assured* me he had many straight (and solvent, Praise Jesus) male clients. I was skeptical of his holiday scheme, but he insisted. So, against my better judgment, hope blowing in the wind, I went. The party was populated with gay men, straight women, and gay hairdressers. What was I thinking? I had a better chance of meeting a straight guy at the Gay Pride Parade.

I signed up for a day of adventure with some group (run by a woman) with a name like "New York Adventures." You could buy a day. This particular day came with many enticements for me, Valerie: swimming in a creek, horseback riding, wine tasting, and a visit to a local ice cream shop. Yup, a day in the country splashing, cantering, slurping, and licking. I have no idea where we were. It could have been Connecticut, Jersey, or upstate New York. It's all the same to me unless I'm driving. And I don't drive. I was excited for this day, the fact of getting out of my house and my selfsame weekend routine as a divorcee: the gym, a rollerblade in the park, a movie rental, and bed. Woo, hoo. I am neither night crawler nor bar hop.

So I met up with this group on the Upper West Side at Starbucks. I was nervous, wary, but hopeful, just like when I went to the hairdressers' party in the West Village. You can see where I'm going with this. I'm sure you're two steps ahead of me.

I arrive at Starbucks to find…a bunch of women. How delightful. Now, I love women. I love women, *really*. I'm demonstrative and tomboyish, just shy of butch, and I've been accused of being gay, mostly by my paranoid mother, who also accused me of being a drug addict when I told her I tried pot, once. Go, Mom. She was watching too much *Donahue* in those days. However, I am straight and I was looking to meet a guy.

There was *one* guy there. He was cute. *Really* cute, and accompanied by his girlfriend, who was equally cute. My heart sank. I wasted money. I was wasting time. This day was a complete bust. Now I had to do all these "fun" things by myself, or rather, with a bunch of girls like I was twelve years old again and at camp, but with wine. Big fucking deal. I would never get married. I don't even like Starbucks. But I'd pre-paid, so off I went to Connecticut, upstate New York, Jersey, Pennsylvania or wherever the hell it was. There were trees. This indicated I had left the Isle of Manhattan.

We went horseback riding first. It was a beautiful summer day, sunny but not too hot. I'm no expert horsewoman but I am a huge horse lover, a decent athlete, and have enough experience on a horse (one hour every ten years) to make me feel like a pro. I'm sure it's past life recollection of Indian and Cavalry experience that brings it all back. In fact, when I was teeny tiny (now I'm just tiny, not teeny, at just under five feet—who has time to say "four feet eleven and three quarters"? I'm five feet tall and sticking with it) I desperately wanted a horse, and when I say desperately, I mean I bugged my mom *mercilessly*.

My mother said, "Where would we put it?"

What kind of a pedestrian question was that? She was not a *visionary*, like I am.

I recall having a nightmare when I was around five or so. It was so vivid the images and associated trauma are still clear to me. My horse had gone over a cliff and I was devastated. I woke up crying. His name was two syllables, like "Lightning" or "Midnight." I said, "Lightning went over the cliff!!!! Lightning went over the cliff!!!! Lightning went over the cliff!!!" I was hysterical and could not stop sobbing. My mother, who *taught* me to believe in reincarnation (as did my dad) poo-pooed it as "just a dream." How uninspired.

I know now that this was past life recall, past life trauma rearing its ugly head. I still remember the pain of that loss and have summoned it just now, generating a coupla tears. Boo, hoo. My poor Lightning. Did I go over the cliff with him and have repressed that memory? I think not. The feeling was of losing him, not my life. We were partners. Mates. (I was going to say I'm an equiphile, but it turns out that equiphiles like to have sex with horses. That's not love, that's rape. I guess I'm an old-fashioned horse lover. Animal lover. Whatever).

My mother's refusal to buy me a horse in midtown Manhattan was both cruel and capricious. I even tried campaigning for a *mini* horse. She was intractable. *She* rode horses, for god's sake. She belonged to a riding club and cut a gorgeous figure as a young horsewoman in Central Park.

My mother said that horses were stupid and dangerous. How rude. How insulting. Why did she ride them? She was on a horse one day when she felt someone grab her left shoulder. It was the horse behind her. He had wrapped his yellow teeth around her tiny shoulder. What's dumb about that? Maybe he thought she was cute. Maybe he was hungry. Maybe he wanted her to move up and get out of his way.

Horses are obstinate. So am I. Does that make me dumb? No, it does not. She claimed her horse would not leave the stable one day no matter what she did to coerce him. The entire ride was an unbearable battle as he struggled to get back to the stable. She found out later that her horse had not been fed. That horse was a genius. I wouldn't leave without lunch, either. For god's sake, those animals didn't even get paid. No lunch, no work. Union!!!

Then there was the day that her horse reared and went absolutely nuts in the park. Turns out a horse had been shot after an injury and died right there. Her horse had reacted to the spirit activity (a murder, no less). This is not stupid. He, like all animals, was a medium. "They shoot horses here, don't they? Get me out!" Whoa, Nelly.

My mom had horse prejudice. Even if she did love them. Any horse whisperer or psychic knows that they, like all animals, have a genius all their own. It is humans who are pig-headed (sorry, pigs are smart), humans who are often small-minded, stupid, close-minded, and egotistical. Animals are connected to the Omnibrain, the All That Is. Ain't no stupid there. Humans, with free will, have chosen Paris Hilton like solipsism, and reality show inanity. It isn't pretty. I'd rather a horse for president than George Bush. (He wasn't president anyway, that was Cheney, the Dark Horse/Ring Wraith, assisted by Sauron (Rumsfeld) and Saruman (Wolfowitz) and their small cabal of ne'er do wells). I am not maligning all humans. Just the ucky ones.

So I'm out in the country on adventure day on my horse, Candy. Nice enough horse, though she was perhaps a bit standoffish. One of the other horses had an eyepatch and some bruises. This was remedial horseback riding. As is the norm with these beginner horse rides, we meandered at a molasses like clip. It was "Ready, set—snooze." I *walk* faster than those horses moved. I needed to go to Jersey for this? Yawn. We got to the creek and did a little "swimming" (in 12 inches of water, as I recall). Me, the girls, and the one cute guy. With his girlfriend. This day was a huge success. I wasn't miserable due to my love of nature, horses, ice cream, and wine. But I signed up to meet men. My bad.

We got back on our horses, still wet, and as Candy clomped along I realized, "Jesus Christ, even my *horse* is a girl!" How dispiriting. Don't get me wrong, I'm all for the fair sex, I've spent most of my life with it. But I've got myself and that's enough. This day of adventure, intended to bring me closer to meeting and mating with a member of the *opposite* sex, was a complete and total failure. I was in female detention, in an unofficial, ambulatory equine nunnery.

I am drawn inexorably toward those mysterious creatures called men, the ones I've barely known having grown up with neither father nor brother. When I've known them carnally, there was plenty of non-carnal (i.e., personality) gunk that got in the way. That's my karma, my issue, learning the balance between male and female, first within myself, then within the context of a relationship. When you're balanced and whole you've got a good shot at attracting a similar partner. When you're out of balance (that's most of us) look at your partner as a mirror and suck it up. Don't blame. Get to work.

Well, I've got a little spice in me, and so, apparently, had Candy. I couldn't handle the lumbering pace of the geriatric crowd (not the girls but their candy-ass attitude). A few of the more advanced riders cantered off and I kicked Candy so that we could, too. Who gave a shit? I was single and bored. What the hell. I may not get laid, but I'd get a buzz. Candy raced off like a bat out of hell, god bless her. Apparently she was bored with this plodding ruse, too. I was thrilled. Until my left foot dislodged from the stirrup.

I bounced wildly up and down in the saddle, my left leg hurtling in the air, my right foot scraping painfully against the single stirrup, heart racing, adrenaline pumping. Yes, I'd been in this position before (the result of my massive past life horse expertise coupled with little current life experience, and my "the spirit is willing but the flesh is weak" skill set).

I could hear squeals of concern from the sissy riders behind me. Candy and I forged ahead. She chose her course and veered left into a field where the advanced riders were. She wanted to run free. I understood. One of the trail leaders tried to catch up to us but I was able to get Candy under control before something untoward happened to me. I got off of the horse and that was that. I got my cheap thrill. Candy got hers. This was a day (and a liaison) that neither of us would acknowledge again, a sort of "one-ride-stand." I haven't seen Candy since.

My lesson for the day? Adventure groups led by women lead to...more women. Ice cream, wine, swimming, and horses, apparently powerful woman magnets. I guess beer, burgers, drag racing, and golf would have snagged the guys. But that's not me. And I gotta be me.

What did I learn? That I like to ride fast. I like a rush. I even like a little bit of danger, maybe a lot. That I want a cute guy who could go for horseback riding, swimming, and wine (you can nix the ice cream, I'm off white sugar now). What did *you* learn? That I don't know the difference between Jersey, New York, and Connecticut (to paraphrase Gertrude Stein, "A tree is a tree is a tree"). If I'm not in Manhattan, it's a wash. And that whenever I've tried to artificially meet a guy, it's slapped me in the ass, just like Candy.

CHAPTER 14

Sacred Geometry

I am not a math person. I'm not big on numbers. I'm from Dictionopolis, not Digitopolis (please, *please* read *The Phantom Tollbooth* by Norton Juster if you haven't already, or haven't recently. It just celebrated its fiftieth year in print and is a "children's classic" profound enough to set any adult straight. The meaning of life is right there in that brilliant book).

I held my own mathematically in school, working very hard to do so. I got my SAT math numbers up sufficiently to not distract too terribly from my promising English indicators. But as soon as I had satisfied basic math requirements in high school (and I do mean basic, there was no calculus for me) I was done. It was philosophy and theater that compelled me to do and take more. These were mother's milk to me. Math was sandpaper. Sand in my bathing suit. A shard of glass (anywhere).

Nonetheless, I wanted to go to M.I.T. My big sister was a freshman there when I was nine and I was dazzled by the place. Cambridge was magic and I loved the brilliance in the air; the mad genius walking the paths of the campus. There was my sister's wild and wacky male friend (I don't remember his particular genus of genius) whose mother was a beautiful long-haired yoga guru in Boston with her own TV show, and was married to a morbidly obese M.I.T. professor. And how could I forget the guy in my sister's co-ed dorm who rigged the pinball machine in the hallway so I could play pinball at length for free? He was My Knight In Shining Armor. The campus was brimming with brilliance and I wanted in. The only problem was, I was no good at science or math.

I boldly interviewed at the school anyway, interrogating my interviewer. "Don't you have a drama department? And what about philosophy?" I had a plan. "Well, couldn't I just major in drama and philosophy and *not* do any science or math? No? You're positive? That's your final answer? Bummer."

I ended up at a well-known school down the road from my sister's alma mater that had a rigorous and varied curriculum. There were required classes you could pass out of if you were proficient in the subject. Like language. While I'm a master of dialects and can effect a superb pronunciation of the few words I do know (which is why the French in France find me *très charmante*, because while my syntax may be upside down and inside out, my pronunciation *c'est parfait*.) I was not strong enough in French to pass out of the language requirement, even after three years of high school French. I was convinced that learning languages had something to do with math (those declensions were just so, so...*orderly*).

One of my high school French teachers was from France. He had thick, rectangular, black-framed glasses, the de rigueur beret, a comprehensive proboscis, a threadbare comb-over, and an unmerited diva-like demeanor. As bumbling and "étrange" as Inspector Clouseau, he was obsessed with wealth and repeatedly referenced Chateau d'Yquem wine in class (I just priced it online and found one bottle for $719.00 and another for $789.00). When I asked him how I could improve my French grade, he said slowly and point blank with his thick French accent, "Buy—me—macadamia—nuts." Seeking actual academic insight and improvement, I did not accede to his bribe request. My grade remained "adéquat."

I didn't even bother to attempt to "pass out of" my college language requirement. As a result, I had to take a foreign language freshman year. I chose Modern (Demotic) Greek as I am half-Greek and happen to love the language. I can read it slowly, sort of, and now know a few words beyond the "baklava" and "galatoboureko" that I learned at the hands of my mother. The class was impossibly hard for me, though I was so proud to share with my mother what I was learning, and she was so thrilled to hear me speak full sentences out of my workbook. "Mr. and Mrs. Pavlakis have a vase of flowers on their table." (Yes, I can still say this in Greek). Honestly, if I didn't know how to tell jokes in English, I don't think I would have passed the class in Greek (I think I got a D, if I was lucky). Learning language, it turns out, is strongly connected to math skills. Forming sentences requires a "formula" with proper structure (why, it's practically scientific). While my romantic heart yearned for beautiful lilting sounds to trip off of my tongue, the need for weighty, accurate declensions grounded me to a mute earth.

College philosophy proved similarly frustrating for me. It wasn't the dreamy philosophizing that adhered to my love of religion, spirituality, and metaphysics. No, my freshman philosophy class involved impossible forms of reasoning, including deductive and inductive, all of which remained inscrutable to me. There was that math again! Damn logic. I was locked out of the love of wisdom castle (love of wisdom is the literal translation of "philo" love and "sophia" wisdom). I switched out while I was inexorably behind. Another mental strike against my heart-felt passions.

The other requirement one could pass out of freshman year was Quantitative Reasoning. Those very words froze my bohemian blood. They were alien code. I assiduously cracked my Q.R. study books the summer before freshman year. My mother even had to *buy* the study books, adding insult to injury for something I wanted nothing to do with. I attempted to discern the charts and graphs. They were worse than Greek to me. I got jittery just looking at the unopened books lying on the floor. They represented a form of death to me. Quantitative kryptonite, they melted the chocolate bunnies in my heart.

There were two parts to this Q.R. requirement, one more traumatizing than the next—statistics and computer *programming* (this was in the '80s and, so, *way* ahead of the PC curve). I might as well have been at M.I.T. majoring in Aerospace and Biomedical Engineering. Most of my peers immediately passed out of Quantitative Reasoning when they jumped off the boat freshman week. When I got to campus, I dutifully signed up for the prep class with the six other math retards in my freshman class of 1,600 apparent statistical, computer, and math geniuses. I studied long and hard to make the grade. I sweated. I tore my hair out. I stared at the inscrutable charts again and tried to make sense out of what seemed *anything* but reasonable to me. The moment I had been preparing for all summer arrived. I took the test. It was an hour. There were twenty questions. Passing was eighteen. Everyone passed. Except me. I got sixteen.

I signed up for the prep course *again* and took the test. Again. This time, I was given an ample hour and a half extending the excruciating torture session (allegedly out of "kindness" but obviously out of consideration for my "handicap."). Passing was lowered to sixteen. I got fourteen. I figured if I tried a third time they'd give me nine hours to retake the test; a bowl of oatmeal, honey, and warm milk; and tutors on either side to lovingly "prompt" me. Passing would be twelve. I'd get seven. Having failed a second time, I was thus consigned to hard labor. I registered for the semester long Quantitative Reasoning class. I had a nice young teaching assistant (probably some math genius Ph.D. candidate). I studied ardently (you *know* I also needed extra explanatory study sessions with teacher, right?) and I eventually passed the course. I still have no idea what Quantitative Reasoning is.

But my favorite math teacher was Yves Volel at my high school in New York City. He was bigger than life, at over six feet tall, and had a personality to rival The Sun. He was a slightly pigeon-toed, well-dressed, garrulous Haitian man with a bit of a tummy, nice, shiny black shoes, a French accent, and a lisp. He was my geometry teacher and the best thing about him was he rarely talked about geometry. He talked about Haitian politics. He was divorced from Baby Doc's daughter, happily remarried, and had a young daughter. He babbled about his daughter all the time. He was so proud of her.

He was the head of a movement he'd started called Operation EXODUS, to help liberate his country. Since he was opposing the reigning government, there were attempts on his life. He told us all about these attempted murders in class. I was riveted. A large rock was dropped on his windshield as he was driving off a New York bridge. Gas was piped into his apartment, nearly killing him, his wife, and daughter. The other kids thought he was crazy, but I believed him. Why not? Duvalier was a bad guy and politics is frequently a deadly business. Mr. Volel went on and on with the stories. But best of all, the more he talked about Haiti, the less he talked about geometry.

He riffed on various topics. He went on one day about the delicacies of the human body. "If you have too much salt in your body, *you die*! If you have not enough salt in your body, *you die*! If you have too much sugar in your body, *you die*! If you have not enough sugar in your body, *you die*! If you have too much heat in your body, *you die*! If you have not enough heat in your body, *you die*!" Life and death were very real issues in my geometry class.

Volel was passionate about everything, from teaching math, to liberating countries, to his wife and child, to photography, to his students. He talked poetically (and privately, to me) about the injustice of grades, how "this A, this B, this C, this D…the teachers don't realize how they affect the student for *the rest of his life*." This speech was probably inspired by my asking him how I could improve my geometry grade. I think I got a B+. No macadamia nuts.

His love of people and of life was palpable as he walked the halls and enthusiastically took candid photos of the teachers and students, filling our yearbooks with his work. He took a shot of me lying stomach down, feet flopped up on a bare mattress in the school theater, and another shot sophomore year in front of the school gate, wearing jeans, Frye boots, and a camel-colored swing coat with brown suede elbow patches. He was a kind man and took a special interest in me, perhaps because he knew my father was dead. I loved him.

In September of 1987, true to his word, Yves Volel was back in Haiti, running for President. He held a press conference in front of police headquarters. He lifted up the Haitian Constitution in one hand and his law degree in the other. (Who knew my math teacher was a lawyer?). He was publicly defending a man who had been illegally arrested, detained, and beaten. Yves was rushed by undercover cops shouting, "Long live Volel for President! Long live Volel for President!" The cops pushed him, shot into the air, then shot him repeatedly in the neck and chest. My math teacher was assassinated.

The crowd panicked and dispersed. His body lay alone, face down, untouched on the ground for an hour. He was 52. The story ran on the front page of the New York Times.

So much for the nay-sayers in my high school who mistook Mr. Volel's passion for righteousness and freedom for mere madness. Perhaps those kids were satisfied with how good they were at math.

Occasionally in class Mr. Volel would show us a math theorem. When he finished it he joyously sang a little ditty. He pointed with the chalk at the board, beaming like a kid at Christmas at the beautiful answer. "Ba, da, da, di, di, da!" he sang.

Ask any Haitian cab driver in New York City who Yves Volel is, and he will tell you.

CHAPTER 15

Mama Rules

I recently saw *Mama, I Want to Sing*, a show that started in East Harlem, New York City, in 1983. I recall the TV ads featuring dizzyingly high soprano notes reminiscent of Minnie Riperton's (she sang "Loving You" in 1975) vocal gymnastics. It's nearly thirty years later and "Mama" is still alive, now in West Harlem.

This is not a show I would normally go to. In my mind, it was by and for black people, and while I love gospel, and black people, I would not have sought the show out. Full disclosure, even as a performer, there's very little theater I seek out. Ticket prices are high, among other concerns. Having seen a lot of bad theater (or theater that just plain doesn't speak to me) is the other part of my "stay at home" equation.

I used to be moved by theater when I was a kid. Broadway dazzled. It was the gold standard when I was in high school. It was special. It was cool. Sophomore year I sobbed all the way home after seeing Richard Gere and David Dukes in *Bent*, a drama about homosexual love (and duh, death) in a Nazi concentration camp. Now, Broadway is overwhelmingly commercial, filled with pyrotechnics, video effects, and sky-high ticket prices. Thanks, I'll just stay at home and knit a sweater (not). It's not all bad by any stretch. I just don't have the $400 required to see the one or two shows that even vaguely intrigue me. Theater is meant to be cathartic, to take you on an emotional journey and offer insights and release. "Mama" took me on just such a journey.

I was offered a ticket by a friend. Wondering about the schlep (I don't get up to Harlem, either west or east, that often) I accepted since it was both free and an adventure of sorts. The only thing I stood to lose was my time.

The Dempsey Theater is housed in a retired public school. The building is old. West 127th Street is old. History is in the air. I used the kiddie bathroom then joined the hordes of folk settling into their seats. I looked around. Black folk, yes. A coupla honkies (that would be me, I'm proudly un-pc, and I don't have the time or inclination to cough out "Caucasian"). There were Japanese kids. Black kids. Black seniors. Whatever I am (a short, Greek, German, tap-dancing person).

The show is a rousing experience, the music uplifting. Want to reach heaven? Sing! Gospel music *is* joy personified. That's how to worship, *celebrate*. Fill yourself with the spirit, *embody* the spirit. The performers were replete with *enthusiasm* (which means "filled with God" from the Greek "en-theos." Theos/Deus means God). The voices were all magnificent.

Not a classical theater experience (it's mostly singing, with some talk), I liken the show to a journey. You have to flow with the river of emotion. It's not just about a young girl's passion for singing. It's about passion for life, love, and family.

I cried when (lead) Doris's preacher daddy died. Her family egged her to move on, and when she finally relented, I was moved by that, too. Doris evolves from a little girl in pigtails to a young lady finding her expression as a soulful singer.

Vy Higginsen wrote this story (with her husband) about her late sister, Doris Troy, whose big hit was the 1960's "Just One Look." Vy, a gorgeous woman and former radio personality, narrates the story and is on stage the whole time. She is so entirely wrapped up in the production that she often mouths the words and even shadow boxes as young Doris battles with her mama for her right to go out into the world.

At show's end, Vy filled us in on the fact that the young lady playing her late sister Doris Troy is her only daughter. The show is a celebration of family, and this is exemplified by the spirit among cast and audience.

I didn't watch the Oscars this year. I gave up television three years ago, mainly for budgetary reasons, but also because I'm not too keen on what's generally pumped out of the idiot box. But right there at the Dempsey Theater, I got to *see* the Oscars, because Vy Higgonsen thanked *everyone* in the audience. The more she thanked, the more I loved her. The theater was oozing with gratitude, joy, and love.

AARP, The Fashion Institute of Technology, and a teenage Japanese tour group was in the house. There were kids joining Vy's "Gospel for Teens" group for their first rehearsal after the show. We were all family. Black, white, Japanese, young, old, you name it. Gospel, God, and an appreciation of art, dance, and music brought us together. *This* is the New World Order, not the fearful 1984 scenario we've survived and that some bleak folk predict for the future. Happy days are here again because the Goddess is back.

Here are the new rules for the Goddess's return:

Love first.
Follow your passion.
Be inclusive.
Help others.
Let others help you.
Feel your sacredness.
Be the blessing to others.
Love, love, and love some more.
Say thank you.
Sing, dance and celebrate!

As I left the theater I congratulated Vy on the show, and the producer (her husband) asked me what I liked most about it. I wasn't just revenue to him. And it wasn't just me. He and Vy talked to as many people as they could as they departed.

"I loved that the show exemplifies community, dreams, and family," I said. I felt virtually hugged as I left the theater, and when I saw some of the performers in the school stairwell afterward, I complimented them on their beautiful work.

Vy endeavors to bless and enrich Harlem, her home. She wants to bring Harlem back to its cultural glory of old. She is blooming where she was planted, watering and nourishing her garden by keeping the art form of gospel alive in the hearts and souls of young performers. Her garden is flourishing.

I will close by quoting/paraphrasing Dr. Patch Adams' 12-minute YouTube ode to the transformative healing power of Mama.

"My brother and I work for love because of our mother. She showed us the miracle of being nice, of being kind, of being generous *as a way of life*. This did not make me political until I grew up and realized that *her* world was not *the* world.

"At the age of eighteen I began a revolution for loving and it was easy to do because my mother gave me self-esteem. She made me know if I decide something, I can do it.

"No medical school in the world teaches compassion. But long before I go to medical school I see a world that is serious. I started to clown everywhere because the adult world was serious, oppressed by this global idea that money and power *over others* is god. And, so, when I go to medical school I start a hospital that is free, where everyone is equal, where you have a lot of time with patients, you live with the patients, you have art, these are the ideas I was working with, not just clowning.

"The playful way I dress is part of the message to put joy in the public space. It is to connect people. We can *teach* people to be revolutionaries for loving change. To move away from market capitalism and to a world of compassion and generosity.

"I don't have pain for me. I have pain for humanity. Today, 30,000 children will die of starvation. And tomorrow. And this is not interesting. *Football* is interesting. *Hair* is interesting. *Shoes* are interesting. But hungry children, not interesting. Twenty to fifty million men a day have sex with a child. Dirty air, dirty water, destroyed environment, this is not interesting. I do not focus on the pain of this, to go "oh god, this is terrible. I say, how can it *change*? *How* can we change it?

"I live in paradise with my friends, doing work for love. I live in a planet that for me is paradise. But I am aware that if we don't change to a loving world, there is no hope for human survival. I'm 64, so I'm on the "dessert" phase of my life; for the rest of my life it's like ice cream. A nice tart. But for your children, grandchildren, and great grandchildren I see no life unless we change.

Don't hold the pain. Use it as stimulus. Let's work joyfully to change.

"It is no secret; women for all of history have been doing what we need. All the problems of the world are due to men. You can't name one problem in history due to women, no matter how bad men behave with their wars and their greed and their nasty acts, no matter how badly they behave, the women are raising the children.

"And so, we only have to act like…did you have a sweet mother? We only need to act like *your mother*. Did you have a sweet grandmother? We only need to act like *your grandmother*. So it's not a big thing, 'Jesus must come! Patch Adams must come!' This is crap. 'Mama!' All we need is *Mama*. What mama brings with her, 'Does everybody have *food*? Would you like some more food? Look, your hair, let's brush your hair a little bit. Ah…your clothes, they need to be cleaned. Let's go next door and help the family next door.'

"We need Mother/Grandmother Revolution. I live it. And I invite *you* to live this dream. Hear me. There is no hope for human survival if we don't change to a loving world. There's no hope for rich people in the future, no hope for *anybody*, if we don't make a world whose values are compassion and generosity."

I now quote from *The Crow* (a favorite flick of mine) oh heck, I just looked it up and *they* got it from the original author, William Makepeace (Make Peace, great name, huh?) Thackeray: "Mother is the name for God in the lips and hearts of little children."

This is the world I want to create, where everybody celebrates with song, says, "Thank you," "I love you," and "Let me help you." It takes a family to raise a planet. God bless the Goddess. The Divine Feminine. She is here to stay. She lives within us all. Praise love and long live Mama.

CHAPTER 16

The Hand Off

Why was I so sad last week? It could have been the galactic energies hitting the earth. We are receiving massive doses of heightened spiritual energy cleansing and clearing out the old density of sadness, grief, patterns of negativity, anger, jealousy, etc., to make room for the increased energies of love, joy, and freedom starting to rule the planet. (It *is* the dawning of the Age of Aquarius, after all.) It could have been hormones. It could even have been the impending date of my beloved (dead) mother's birth, September 13. More to the point, it was probably a combination of all these things, and then some.

But the most immediate culprit for my despondency was the imminent wedding of a friend of mine. Oh, not a close friend, not by a stretch. Someone I take class with at the gym. But she's a peer, of sorts, if a few years younger than I am. I'd heard her whine about men, she'd heard me do the same, but less so, since I didn't really date, and she did. She's a bit of a yenta, a bit of a whiner, but pretty, and, someone decided to purchase the package. There were but eight or ten months between their first date and the wedding, though the fellow, a divorcee with kids, had had her number for years before actually calling her.

I was jealous on every count, including the speed and ease of the union and its celebration, the wedding at her parents' house on the beach, and the very fact that she had parents. That, too, was a luxury to me since mine were long gone. I already had one (crap) wedding with no 'rents (of mine) in the house. It's a nice touch, parents at the party. Especially if you happen to like yours, as I did.

I wasn't inordinately jealous at first. In fact, despite my petty malaise, I sent her a warm but brief congratulatory email five days before the wedding, wishing her the happiest of days and a wonderful honeymoon. It was something she could easily have responded to with a mere three letters back, such as, "Thx!" She did not. So much for my being "big." I went right back to being small.

Given the location of her parents' home, there was a good chance they were quite wealthy. In fact, I heard the mother of the bride was selecting the diamond, if not the very ring, which I found rather fulsome. However, she was still one diamond, one groom, one wedding, and two parents ahead of me. Go Team Bride.

While the day before was stormy and the same was predicted for The Big Day, the bride and I awoke to the most glorious of days—she in her boudoir, me in my bachelorette pad flanked by cat, dog, and coffee cup. The weather was preternaturally gorgeous. It exceeded expectations, indeed, it was practically a work of art, something cinematographers and painters long to capture or fabricate. Heavenly, summery sun with a wisp of fall in the air, it was warm with a cool breeze. The brilliance of light blazed through leaves while wind animated sublime, puffy clouds. This egregiously gorgeous day was something you couldn't buy even if you could afford it. And she could. Cool, crisp, and stunningly lit, it was one for the books. There were no two ways about it. This was a good day to get married.

What kind of attempted shadenfraude lurked within me, you ask? I'll tell you. Despite the glaring sun and perfect skies, I secretly wished it would still rain, as the forecast had predicted. What does this say about me? I'm not even close with the girl. So what was this massive malaise about? I'm still trying to figure it out. Out loud. With you. There was no rain, nor satisfaction to be had for me that day. It was resplendent from beginning to end. She won.

What did I do that day? Well, since no one asked me to get married, I rehearsed a play in a friend's back yard early in the morning. I was with very nice people, in a very nice yard, reading a very good play. I kept staring at the sky, the flowers, the trees, and the birds. Oh, to be out in the country. Out in nature. I long to be in nature, but if I had to be in the city, I was in the right spot on a Sunday morning. It was sublime. The very day was sublime. But I wasn't living my life. I kept thinking about what "she" was doing, she with her family, her dress, her home by the ocean. What luck this bride seemed to have. Two dates. Boom. Marriage. I guess the glaring question slapping me in the face was, "Where's my luck?" Except that I don't believe in luck. So whom do I blame, myself? I come to intermittent peace regarding my solitary status, but that doesn't mean I don't still "want it all." In fact, I've "wanted it all" for decades now. The marriage/family brass ring remains elusive yet.

Even the director of the play I was doing is getting married in a month. Two other gym friends recently pushed out babies. I felt again (as I do every ten years or so) that life was passing me by. Let me not forget to add that the very strong prospect of delivering (via C-section) a bouncing baby (benign) fibroid tumor (or 2 or 7) awaits me in the near future. It was all of a piece, and all too much for me on this beautiful day. I wanted to cry. So I did.

On the prettiest day of the year, with people getting married, having babies, having brunch on the upper west side with their strollers, dogs, husbands, iPhones, and kids, I walked home alone. Actually, I took the bus because I was hungry (it would have taken an hour to walk). Took only 45 minutes by bus! By God, I was making progress.

Let me also add that the benign growths have been affecting my period, which is quite late. Between the factors of being premenstrual for a month and the size of the growths, I myself looked pregnant. Not in a good way. Couple this with the fact that the day before the wedding was the last day of my three-month subscription with an online dating service. Overall, the experiment had been a very expensive bust; despite the one pleasant date I had with a pleasant man with whom I shared absolutely no chemistry. It was the first (and last) time I'll blow money on a dating website. My foray into the murky world of online dating had netted nothing but nothing. Phooey.

When I realized I had been completely suckered in on this website by the rash of cute guys who wrote me immediately (after I paid), but never followed up (at the point I could no longer get a refund), then once again, on the *very* day my membership expired (requiring a new influx of cash from me) a new rash of emails poured in after three months of silence, I was convinced it's a scam designed to lure you in and lure you back. It's that manipulative computer "algorithm" shit. They electronically "stir the pot" when you first join, making your profile prominent, and then again, when they're about to lose you. In the middle I had virtually no activity. La di da.

Do people meet on this website? Absolutely, I know two or three couples who met on this exact website and are now married or living together. Does that mean the service doesn't play "Three-Card Monty" with the rest of us? No it does not. Online dating is the "Vegas of Matchmaking." You pays your money and you takes your chances. Taking advantage of lonely-hearts is like taking financial advantage of a grieving family when they are planning a funeral. I had my mother cremated simply and I did not renew my online membership. Those 11 emails will just have to sit there and wait for some other sucker to read them.

My mood shifted from sad to mad when I got an email from a real pal, writing about her all too real (read "troubled") marriage. I gave her advice, insight, my incendiary perspective (as is my wont), and fired the Molotov cocktail off, wondering if it would shock, appall, give the girl a heart attack, or send her screaming for the hills not from him, but from me. I found that in the process of responding to what sounded like her extreme emotional abuse, I myself got angry. On her behalf? Perhaps. I love this girl. She was a college roommate and is one of the dearest, kindest people I know—smart, funny, loving, a good mom, a great friend, and a loyal wife, married to a depressed and angry man who rides her like the devil.

Was I reliving some angst from my own "skewed" marriage in which I attempted to dispense honey and received continual, ample doses of vinegar in exchange? Sure. Did it fire up all the disgust and frustration welling up and raging in me as I confront my current challenges: lack of partner, family, and concerns about income and health? Did my future rise ominously like a black tidal wave threatening to swallow me up? Yes it did. My deepest fears menaced, that I would die alone, impoverished, sealing the fate of these last decades in which I have survived without parents, mate, family, or kids. One in which I have managed to get by, financially, with odd jobs, while income from my true loves (spirituality, acting, and writing) had eluded me. What conclusions was I to form from all of this? That I am alive, sane, solid, centered, a tough cookie. And occasionally really, really pissed off.

I left my house to perform the play I had rehearsed the day prior (on the Gym Bride's infamous Day of Glory). The play was about mothers of daughters, and daughters of daughters. I had experience in one of these departments, having had an intense relationship with my own mother. I was to play both daughter of a mother and mother to a daughter, the monkey in the middle. I was weepy as I left my house, fear and frustration roiling within. I saw a bus approach as I neared the stop. I'd have to run to make it. I waffled, and then ran for it.

As I got closer and noted the crowds both on and off the bus, waiting to get on, waiting to buy tickets on the sidewalk, I weighed the benefits of being on time versus being comfortable. I like to read the uplifting, channeled *Sedona Journal of Emergence* when I commute, particularly when I'm deflated. I needed to nourish myself and this would not be possible on a packed rush-hour bus. So I slowed to a stop just as I reached the madding crowds. Emerging from the throng, a pretty, petite brunette in her 30s or 40s approached me silently. She had taken in my situation in a flash—my eyeing the bus, the crowd, the line to buy a ticket, my defeated slow to a stop. She silently flicked a small piece of paper in my face, discreetly and delicately between her index and third fingers. It was her ticket, neatly folded twice, and it would serve as mine. We were face to face for a millisecond. I took the ticket, and, acknowledging her kindness with my eyes, followed the white rabbit and proceeded on to the packed bus. The operation was illegal, silent, seamless, and filled with the milk of human kindness and divine intervention. Within a minute I was further blessed with a seat and was able to comfortably read.

I went on to give a moving performance and though it took an hour to get home via bus, the night was filled with peace. This was my life. Me. The moon. Alone together, brimming with the poignancy of my full heart and emotions. My longing. Myself. I could handle the silence. Indeed, on one level I loved it and always had. That is the quandary of being me—a lover of silence and solitude on the one hand, with a yearning to love and be loved by a partner on the other.

Over the next week my emotions continued to brew and I allowed an assortment of triggers to set me off. I became irritated by own habit of being too friendly, accommodating, and accessible, even while walking my dog. Do I *have* to talk to everyone? Sometimes I don't want to, nor do I want my clean dog to be sniffed by dirty dogs, nor to engage in "shit chat" with owners of said mangy dog owners who piss their energy away with endless empty musings on important topics such as "the weather." I became mad as hell (at what? who cares) and I wasn't going to take it anymore. I became sullen.

When a chatty, clingy perv in my exercise class jumped up and down in joy when he saw I'd (unknowingly) set my mat right next to his, he accused me of trying to "cuddle" with him and cheekily suggested he "wasn't sure he was going to allow it."

I turned dark as a storm cloud and replied, "I wouldn't call it cuddling." Even *that* was me being "nice," for what I really wanted to say was, "You are a pervert and a pest. Piss off."

I've been sick of this dude for months now, but I've yet to sass him, though I've given him plenty of glowering looks, none of which have dampened his ardor. As he sidled closer and closer to me during class with his sweaty, hulking mass, I backed farther and farther away, like the cartoon pussycat from Pepe Le Pew. This I'd done before. But then I did something I'd never done. I asked the ladies nearby in this packed class to accommodate me by moving their mats (they understood exactly why) and I moved away from him outright. When he noticed I was gone, he started dancing awkwardly to the music like a fat six year old who has to go to the bathroom, then stared fixedly at someone else. He's like Rick Moranis's character in *Ghostbusters*, forever trying to ingratiate himself with the girls by joking and flirting. He's fat, he's in his 50s, and it's clear he's not there for the workout given his globular physique and his abstention from lifting a single weight of note.

On an enraged roll, I decided to get divorced. Again. Facebook style. My ex-husband (who was barely my friend when we were married and is now "in a relationship" with someone else) had requested my hand in Facebook friendship a few years back. I was amused. He who had recoiled from my attempts at closeness when we were actually married now sought out a jovial "friendship" on the internet. I had accepted and was further amused to see that he "liked" practically everything I did now, something which could hardly be said during our time together as a couple. From there I became "friends" with my former sister and mother-in-law. I was back in the fold. Now, I loved these people at the time I was married, and they were family to me. It was nice to reconnect with them. Homey-like. In an internet sort of way.

But the fact of the matter is, we are *not* family anymore, and Facebook Friends is not the same as Real

Friends anyway, or Real Family. I was sick of this ruse too, of pretending to be "big" and "mature" about the fact that they (five siblings) all have 2-5 kids themselves, their Facebook pages flouting photos of family gatherings, reunions, birthdays, and the fact that my ex has a five year old with a girlfriend 15 years his junior. I clicked "unfriend" three times. Once each for former husband, sister, and mother-in-law. The internet divorce was now complete.

I was gratified until the Catholic girls' school across the street started rehearsing their marching band, complete with tuba, trumpets, triangles and trombones on the sidewalk for all to hear. Given the skyscrapers, the acoustics are terrible, by which I mean LOUD. The sound echoes and amplifies in what amounts to cacophony, for I cannot abide marching bands and those crappy tunes, the very same crappy tunes they played repeatedly last spring, to my horror. There was nothing I could do about the discord but close the window and play my own music. Louder.

A week later to the day of the wedding was another beautiful day. Not *quite* as beautiful as the first, but it was comparable. As I walked my dog I took stock of myself and what I'd accomplished over the prior seven days. I'd been depressed. I'd been annoyed. I'd performed in a play reading, hosted an old friend for a week, relocated away from the pervert at the gym, voted in the primaries and divorced my ex-husband on Facebook. I'd been sullen and grumpy and felt good about it. I'd cried, missed my mom, and carried on.

I thought to myself, alone yet again on this beautiful day, "This is a beautiful day. Wait. This is a beautiful day to *not* get married. It's just a beautiful day." To walk my dog. To do nothing. To be single. To be alone. To breathe. Heck, it's even a good day to die (as the old Indian said to Dustin Hoffman in the movie *Little Big Man*). And I ran with that one. It's a good day *to be depressed*. It's a good day *to be angry*. It's a good day to be any *goddamn thing I want to be*. Why do nice days have to be saved for smiles, romance, ice cream, and marriage? Why can't I do what I want? Feel how I am? Be who I am, when I am, where I am, without judging it as good, bad, appropriate, or inappropriate? I am what I am. Here. Now. There is no imperative, moral or otherwise, to be anything other than that. Even if I am wanting more (like a partner someday) does that lessen who and what I am right now? Not all of us can get married on the beach. Some of us have to walk the dog by ourselves. Is that no reason to celebrate life?

Yes. It's a beautiful day to *not* get married. It's a good day to do anything or nothing at all, to be depressed, even. The perfect day to be happy, sad, annoyed, or homicidal. (I'm not encouraging the act, just, perhaps, the feeling.) Not needing to conquer the world, enjoy the day, "seize" the day, or prove anything to anyone, I decided to stay home and menstruate.

Yes, after a month of waiting, the floodgates finally opened, much to my relief. When I accepted who I was (divorced, not "in a relationship," not even happy, friendly, perky, or hopeful) my body released. Like the coolness of that silent transaction between the stranger and myself at the bus stop, I shook my hand and made a deal with myself. Let it be. Let the river run.

CHAPTER 17

Thanks, But No Thanks

"Hey. Is this Valerie?"
"Yes. Is this John?"
"Yeah. How are you?"

Thus began the scintillating conversation between stranger number one and stranger number two as brought together by the internet, specifically, a dating website.

He was, to my great relief, cute. I cannot tell you the number of Jabba the Huts in varying degrees of dress and undress, with or without hair, education, teeth, the most basic ability to spell, and, God forbid, communicate, who have attempted to "communicate" with me (hint, writing a single word, "Hi," is not a conversation starter).

In contrast, a vast number of fit men in their 40s/50s post photos of themselves on top of Mount Kilimanjaro, at the bottom of the deep blue sea spearing sharks, and on land sparring with bear. To show their loyalty and devotion, they boldly clutch their children, their dogs, and their golf clubs, all while baring their abs. These men are triathletes, iron men, and grand prix winners. They are "successful." They bring to the relationship a dowry of sports cars, motorcycles, mountain bikes, snowboards, boats, and an overabundance of ego. The dating profiles are virtual infomercials: Supermen come to life. Some 1,000 men have viewed my profile in the three months I've been a member of this site. To date, I have had but twenty winks, ten emails, and one date (I refuse to count the guy who stood me up). This, in and of itself, is somewhat perplexing. Am I such a troll that I warrant not even a wee bit of wooing from seemingly normal men? Do they only want supermodels and twelve year olds? I think we all know the answer.

I set the intention before I subscribed: I want to have three good dates with three good men that will instill my confidence in dating and trust in them. I wished for a most benevolent outcome that these dates be pleasant, fun, and beneficial for both of us. My first date qualified. While he was not my dream date, he was pleasant looking and had a career in design (which I happen to like and respect). Because we spoke comfortably on the phone about sundry topics, I was happy to meet him. Our date lasted two and a half hours and was comprised of an easy rapport, nice wine, nibbles, and a pleasant environment. But pleasant isn't the same as engaging. Being passionate about my spirituality, I touched on it so he would know who I am. The topics I raised were beyond his ken. I am clear about presenting my beliefs as an activist, visionary, mystic, and loudmouth, for I will not sublimate who I am to be with a partner. I don't have to hit them over the head, but I need to disclose, just like I'd want to know if someone was a Mormon or Scientologist or Orthodox anything. I haven't hid who I am in the past, but nor was I received in my fullness, and I want to be truly seen and known in all my relationships, particularly my intimate ones. Our chemistry was less fizzy at the end of several hours together than it was at the start, so we ended the date on a light note and that was that. One down. Two to go.

For those of you who have online dated, you know that a phone call trumps an email and meeting in the flesh trumps a phone call in terms of getting to know someone. I've been thrilled to find that a man has verbal and intellectual flair in an email, only to have no further contact with him. Or been pleased to find that someone is really easy to talk to on the phone but again, he has no follow through. I had a 45-minute, first-time conversation with a guy who, on the surface, was not my type, as I am not drawn to Harley guys. However, our effortless telephonic rapport inspired me to feel genuine enthusiasm about meeting him.

We set up a dinner date in my neighborhood. The days leading up to the date were filled with anticipation for me. He stood me up. Oh, not literally; but he cancelled within an hour of the date with some ridiculous bullshit excuse. It was implausible, and I did not believe him. He offered to reschedule. I begrudgingly did. He pulled the same stunt a second time a few days later, with yet another over the top absurd excuse that was a clear lie. He kept trying to reach out to me over time, but I ignored him after the second kick in the ass. Stand me up once, shame on you. Stand me up twice...I was crushed.

Another fellow seemed decent if not ideal. Not quite near me location wise, he was divorced with kids. We set up a date. He cancelled via email as I was en route to the date. Had I not *just* gotten a smart phone that week, I would have taken two buses and travelled an hour to wait for a very rude phantom. I did not believe his excuse either, told him so, and, in fact, he eventually confessed he had cold feet. I wrote back, "If you're too scared to have a first date, then you are not ready for a relationship."

We did try again, and, just like the first yeller feller, he made up a ridiculous excuse for the second date, too (pathological liars have a flair for the dramatic, it's never a splinter, it's a splint on an arm hanging by a capillary). He, too, continued to reach out and make amends, but it was clear to see that the pursuit, the dream, the *fantasy* of meeting was about all these guys could handle. Real date, no. Virtual date, yes. I refused further contact with him as well.

At any rate, without going into full disclosure on my lurid dating history, I will jump to John of Late, whose profile, while fetching (given his good looks) was basic, much to my joy. There were but three photos of him, all fully clothed, one with his dog. He was not snowboarding while making homemade pasta. He was not accepting the Pulitzer while snorkeling. He was straightforward and not, seemingly, a legend in his own mind. When we spoke he said, "I like how simple and direct your profile is. I feel I can be myself with you, and that you will be honest with me."

"You're correct," I said. "I will be honest with you."

He admitted he'd not been in a long-term relationship in five years. No crime there, neither had I. In fact, I think it safe to say, I've been *recovering* from my last long-term relationship, which was volatile and dramatic. I'm not seeking drama anymore. I want peace. My life *is* serene now and I've worked hard to make it that way. I want a man and a relationship that reflect my hard-earned equilibrium, joy, happiness, and contentment.

He offered, "Let me tell you what I like about your profile."

This was novel. This was nice! Someone actually bothered to read what I wrote and attempted to discern the woman behind the words.

"You seem straightforward." Great! Yes I am, and proud of it, too. "You have brown hair." Uh oh. Not so great. I didn't work too hard on that one. "You are petite." My heart started to sink. This was another quality I take no credit for, my being five feet tall to his six-foot-two. "You are in shape," he continued to catalogue as I started to feel not "seen" or liked at all.

I filled in the blanks in my head, "Let me guess. You like that I have eyes?"

John said he missed the intimacy of a relationship. The handholding. The hugging. Uh huh.

"Yes, that's all very nice," I volleyed then turned the conversation toward his job. I asked him what kind of TV producer he was, a job he claimed to love. He responded simply that he'd worked for eleven years on *Good Morning America*, then he asked what I did, which surprised me. Since he'd reached out to me, surely he'd read my simple straightforward profile which listed me as an actress and writer.

I repeated what my profile already said. He did not inquire further about my writing or acting. Given that he's in the arts, and that he was allegedly interested in me, this was also not good.

I turned the conversation toward our dogs. I'd been with mine early that morning in Central Park, where they can go off-leash until 9 a.m., a rare doggie pleasure in New York City. I'd rarely gotten there much before 9, so we'd only have a short while before the leash went back on. I was up at 6 that day and transported my pooch to the park by 7:15. The park was beautiful, sunny, quiet, and, much to my surprise, empty. I figured there'd be lots of early morning New Yorkers, unfettered canines in tow. My dog and I were alone, save for a few stray canines and their unattached humans. John said he never went early to the park because he wasn't awake. (Why not? He worked on *Good Morning America*, not *Saturday Night Live*.) and because his dog Gracie wasn't good off-leash. She just ran off.

I was neither enamored of this fellow nor did I hate him, so when he said, "Are you feeling adventurous? Do you want to meet tonight?" I was pleased.

I really wanted a date since I live a practically cloistered life. This was action. An overture. We could meet, greet, and see if there was anything there. Since we lived near each other I offered, "Do you want to meet in the middle?"

He faltered then countered, "Are we on the same page?"

I was confused. "What do you mean?"

He was silent. I started putting the unspoken two and two together and realized that when this "straightforward" person who valued my honesty said he missed "intimacy" he was referring to sex. When he said, "Are you feeling adventurous?" he meant "Do you want to have sex with me?" Tonight.

I was dumbfounded; "You want to have sex *tonight*?"

He did, though he quickly asserted, "I'm not desperate."

Sure. Right. Then, what *are* you, you rich, pretty boy? Did he think I was desperate because I am four years older than he? Was he targeting older, potential "cougars?" I felt profiled and used, like a blow-up doll on the shelf.

He tried to reassure me. "This won't be just a one-time thing. If I want it once, I'll want it a second time, and a third, and a fourth."

How touching. Maybe after the random, sporadic, serial spawning we could actually go on a *date* sometime. You know, like healthy adults do when they like each other? I don't want someone who wants "it." I want someone who wants "me."

"I am not going to have sex with you tonight," I said. "I don't know you. There's no way I will get to know you sufficiently in one night." I thought about explaining how I *had* had sex on first meeting someone in the past, but that that was my spontaneous decision, I hadn't set out to or agreed to spawn prior to venturing out. But I owed him no explanations. I owed him nothing, in fact. He was trolling for sex with short, brown-haired strangers, with eyes, on a dating website. There are, in fact, websites for just such things and just such men. This was not one of them. I suppose he got away with it with his fancy job and all-American good looks. That and the dog. Here was a guy who dined and dashed, screwed and scrambled, who ran off just like Gracie his dog without her leash. Neither wished to be tethered.

For a man thinking he was forthright in looking to get laid, he was the one who used the euphemism "intimacy," while I discerned his real intent and employed the more accurate term "sex." I called him on his bluff. As he got off the phone he apologized for wasting my time (a full ten minutes).

"I hope you find what you are looking for," I said politely.

"I hope you do, too," he countered.

I hung up, felt stunned for a few minutes, then allowed myself to shed exactly two tears when I didn't know what else to do with my confusion.

What perplexed me next was why I felt so lousy. I didn't know him. His request was no reflection on me. Then why did I feel dirty? Used? Overlooked and uncared for? It didn't take me long to figure out that while I had never been solicited in such a gross and overt manner, I had felt used, overlooked, and unseen in most of my relationships, one way or another. I had loved deeply, and exposed my soul, and received in return, my mates' version of love, which, given the narcissistic sources, didn't extend too far. I don't blame these fellows, though I am comfortable labeling their behavior as heinous. They were doing the best they could, given who they were at the time (dicks). However, with my hard-earned wisdom of the ages I realized I no longer have to date dicks. Whatever karmic draw lured me to their lairs, I've learned that the yearnings of the heart trump the superficial titillations of the ego. These were lessons I had to learn from being in the trenches.

I was surprised when John emailed me a few minutes later. "I feel like a jerk. I'm sorry. Just not into playing games—figure I'd rather be honest about intentions so you can make an educated decision. It's an attempt at being respectful but I think perhaps it came off as crass." He signed with an emoticon sad face. ☹

In fact, one could conclude that soliciting a stranger interested in dating for anonymous sex is both jerky *and* crass. His diversionary use of the word "intimacy" was dishonest, and I'm not quite sure what was "respectful" about any of it. However; I was somewhat relieved by his apology (sort of) and perplexed by it as well. If he's such a cad, why would he feel bad? Why should he apologize for what he unabashedly, and (presumably) does regularly: troll for anonymous sex? I took it as a compliment that he felt remorse or chagrin, for I hadn't chided or chastised. I'd simply declined his offer. And all this from someone who works for such a cheerful, seemingly innocent, bright and sunny morning television show. Just goes to show ya.

Grateful for the opportunity to respond, I wrote, "Yeah, I feel a little weird, too, so thanks for the apology. Your profile doesn't indicate that you just want sex. So if you don't want games, maybe you should be more upfront in your profile. Me, I'm looking for the real intimacy, the kind you get from getting to know, and care for someone. Best, V"

Perhaps this was the cleanest conclusion I could hope for. In looking back, as I do, assessing my past, surveying my present, and contemplating my future, I can see clearly what I want, what I don't want, and stick to my terms because now I like who I am.

CHAPTER 18

A Day In The Country

We've been having a heat wave, in case some of you haven't noticed. It's hot, icky, sticky, humid, ucky, oppressive, and, if you're lucky enough to live in New York City, stinky (rotting garbage and other unmentionables. I won't go on). Where do you go for refreshment if you do not want to soak in your bathtub all day and have lingered as long as you reasonably can in front of an open refrigerator?

I've lived in this city my whole life, and other than a few vacations, a few blessed retreats to other peoples' country homes, a year in Michigan (six full summers at music camp) and four years in Boston for college, I've been stuck in this dump for summers. Don't get me wrong. I love this city. But it's easy to feel like a trapped rat when it's 100 degrees outside and you don't have a "crick" to swim in. Although the East River did splash in my mouth once. I was riding my bike by the river and a huge wave came out of nowhere and doused me. A lot of fun except for the "in my mouth" part. I spat repeatedly. You never know where that water's been. Actually, I do.

On a swelteringly hot day years ago my then husband wanted to go to the beach. I'm not a beach person on a good day. Oh, if you have your own expanse of sand (I hate crowds), cool drinks, and a full umbrella, I'll contemplate joining you. But I have moon-pale skin that the sun delights in burning.

I do not like being hot. I do not like sand in my food. So what's with the beach? I'm more of a lake and creek girl, myself. These bodies of water are less likely to drown one, though I am not afraid of drowning. I can swim all right. But the ocean beat me up once when I was a little kid. I got caught in a wave and it pulled me in, pushed me under, tossed me upside down, slammed me onto the rough ocean floor, forced salty water up my nose, down my throat, and mangled my rag doll body *just* long enough for me to get the point. The Ocean's big. She wins.

So, ex-husband. Beach. The thought of rollerblading (this was our default transportation) to Penn Station on a sweltering day, then taking a hot train out to a hot beach with no reprieve from the burning sun, and oh, all so I could sit around roasting while he played Frisbee with his friends (relentless Frisbee playing on his part was one of my grounds for divorce). Now, I know when you *get* to the beach it *can* be a little better. You go in the water and cool off. There's the occasional breeze. But I would have had to subject myself to so much *more* heat, so much *hotter* heat, for me to get to this "potential" relief that I just couldn't stomach it. Or my marriage.

I have created little refuges for myself over the decades when I'm land-locked in Manhattan. Even though it's an island, we're not blessed with cool breezes or ocean front property. If you go to the edges, you are gifted with sky, water, and the occasional corpse. The subway in summer is hell itself. Heat bounces, blisters, and intensifies between tar and skyscrapers. Manhattan becomes a cauldron bubbling with human lava, its residents reduced to foil wrapped potatoes on hot coals. Everything amplifies, including tempers and the crime rate.

Air-conditioned stores offer momentary relief but do nothing to alleviate one's sense of being stuck in the city. A pal and I ran into a shop recently in heat-stroke desperation. The store's demographic was completely alien from ours. We tried to look natural for a few minutes then resigned ourselves again to our fiery fate outside. In winter I sprint into shops to warm up, in summer I slither in and pretend to shop in order to recalibrate my heat index.

Biking along the edges of Manhattan, down Hudson River Park to Battery Park then up through East River Park, offers freedom and relief. I've learned to take advantage of the fountains and sprinklers in kiddie parks. The kids look on with curiosity at a fully clothed adult dousing herself on her bike. I'm proud to provide them with some deviant adult inspiration.

One restless summer I jumped from rollerblades to bicycle to classes at my gym. As much as I loved my various loops through Central Park or down to the Battery, I still felt like a rat running mazes. I was trying to escape myself as much as the heat. The upside? I got in amazing shape. There are worse forms of stress relief than exercise.

This summer I discovered Roosevelt Island. I can see it from my side of the East River. I noticed a new park being built, a white granite memorial to FDR designed by architect Louis Kahn nearly forty years ago. It's gorgeous, but it won't open 'til this fall. I took the tram over with my little dog since I hadn't been in decades. We had a grand time. It's another world, quiet and peaceful. Roosevelt Island is minimally peopled relative to the five boroughs of New York City. We walked on soft grass under the shade of cherry trees. The river breeze offered comfort, my dog got her squirrel fix, and we cooled ourselves (one of us forcibly) under the garden sprinklers.

I liked it so well when we first went a few weeks ago that I came home, dropped my dog off, and returned immediately with my bike. I was Alice in Wonderland, eager to explore new terrain. There is a Lighthouse at the end of the island, reminding me of childhood trips to Jones Beach and Cape Cod. This trip occurred on a hot, hazy day. I parked and sat alone on the stone wall, surveying the scene. Water, sky, boats, and crying seagulls dimmed the perception that I was in a city. My home was just a hop, skip, and a jump across the river. But it was worlds away.

I photographed the carving on stone posts in front of the Lighthouse. The motif was simple, but esoteric, perhaps Celtic, and decidedly out of place here. I wondered who put it here and why. I proceeded to pick up other peoples' crap and throw it away (I like to leave places better than I find them, so this was my gift to the island). I find myself doing this more and more in Manhattan, too. If everyone took personal and collective responsibility, we'd enjoy a very different world, n'est-ce pas?

I explored a fancy apartment building called the Octagon (the small building attached to the new complex is shaped as such). I wondered if I might want to live in this quiet enclave minutes away from Manhattan, but without the hustle and bustle of the big apple. While the Octagon has been beautifully renovated, it used to be a mental hospital (fun!). Energy carries over, and can leave psychic "imprints." I haven't heard of any ghost stories worse than that their complex was without hot water for a week in winter, but I wouldn't want to be their test case.

Around the back I happened upon their swimming pool. How cool, a swimming pool in New York City!

Upon closer inspection I found it to be of Lilliputian dimensions. It serves hundreds of people, couldn't they make it 4'x6' instead of 2'x4'? When I checked the Octagon rents online, any fantasies I had of living there went out the window. Even if you've got eight sides, a padded wall is a padded wall. Especially if the rent is high. I ain't crazy!

As I got back on my bike and rode a few feet I heard a big baritone voice belt out. Was someone playing opera out their window? A few more yards' ride and I discovered the source of the sound. The Dayspring Church was holding its Sunday morning service. It was tiny, modest and populated by black folk. I was transported to the Deep South with stained glass, singing, heat (temperature), and warmth (human).

As if this didn't already constitute enough magic I found the island's community garden, replete with trellises, hydrangea, and myriad plants. It's hard to fathom that you're in New York City while surrounded by black-eyed susans, watering hoses, and butterflies. I was in Cape Cod, Nantucket, anywhere but here. I left my bike at the gate. It was there when I got back. Apparently there is no crime on Roosevelt Island. Except rampant littering.

Next along the water's edge, the metal prow of a large boat abuts from the sidewalk. This is confusing, but it is from a real boat, all right. This little island was full of surprises. My satchel full of experience, I headed back to the tram to return to Midtown Manhattan.

On yet another long, hot day weeks later I wondered what to do. Stir crazy, I grabbed my bike only to discover that the air was low in my tires. My normal pit stop for air is on the West Side as I head over to Hudson River Park. I contemplated that journey briefly. It meant navigating through long avenues of traffic in the heat, then grappling with many more people, tourists, bikers, runners, bladers, and a two-hour ride. When I'm in the mood, it's fine. It's part of the excitement of New York City. But today I was feeling quiet, and I always listen to my feelings. I took the bike outside. The air was adequate, so I set out on my island adventure.

Though the ride to the tram is but a few blocks, I battled traffic signs, cones, and construction obstructions, necessitating my backtracking several times to get where I was going. Once at the tram, all doors opened magically. There was a cute four-year-old girl with an even cuter male chaperone. He was tender and attentive. She was quite verbal, inquisitive, and utterly unselfconscious. She had skin as pale as mine and sported a lavender shift and purple sunglasses. I was reminded of myself as a little girl, and personally, I envied her escort. The tram operator told them where to find the kiddie park with a sprinkler.

Once on the island I skirted to the south end to visit the new memorial. It's right by an old abandoned (and debilitated) smallpox hospital. There are a lot of hospitals on this island, which was once named Welfare Island. Because of the number of handicapped folk that live there, it was named after FDR since he was handicapped with polio and relied on leg braces and a wheelchair. I gravitated to the sprinklers watering a little bit of grass and a lot of dirt. I don't know what the hell they were trying to hydrate, really. Looked like bad aim to me. I rode through the streams.

I was set loose in Wonderland. The south end was utterly quiet and practically devoid of people. Being alone pleases me, especially in nature. There were butterflies and dragonflies buzzing and zipping by. There were geese by the water and sparrows and squirrels elsewhere. It felt like a nature preserve.

I found the kiddie park with the sprinkler. The little girl and her chaperone were nowhere to be seen. I cooled down for both of us, riding my bike several times through the water, making sure to douse all my angles.

Continuing parallel past the old abandoned coal factory (on yet another small island farther east), I browsed, taking my time as I did my first visit. I wanted to take in all the sights, from the sacred to the profane. Suddenly, a tennis ball on rocks by the water caught my eye. There was a wall with a fence on top to keep people out. I happen to have a small dog obsessed with tennis balls, and there was a brand new ball staring at me. I looked around. The tennis courts were directly across the road. Someone had a strong serve. Seemed such a pity, a brand new ball just sitting there with no one to chew on it. I contemplated skootching under the fence on top of the wall. I looked down at the rocks. The wall was at least four feet tall, possibly five (my height). I could easily get down, but could I get back up? Then, I noticed *another* brand new tennis ball, making this veritable treasure trove even more taunting and tempting. I was hungry for the loot.

Was my dog's soul possessing me? Was she peering through my eyes? But what of the wall, the fence, and the cops? Two of them were nearby in a mini patrol car. I had just asked them if I could get air for my tires anywhere (they mentioned places and streets I didn't know, so that would be a "no" for me). Was this something they'd enjoy arresting me for? They don't have crime here. Perhaps this would make their day; give 'em a little action. After all, I was looking to abscond with their air *and* their tennis balls.

Maybe they wouldn't put me in jail. They could just check me into the Octagon. Crazy bitch. "To climb, or not to climb," over and under, this was the question. Let me add here that we do not *need* tennis balls. We *have* plenty of tennis balls. We have tennis balls galore. But these were contraband, and that added to their allure. I felt like a jewel thief staring at diamonds *just* the other side of the reinforced glass window. I cased the wall again. Too high. I'd be stranded on the rocks, yowling like a cat. My bike would be stolen (the *second* crime on the island). And for what? Dog toys. This was greed, lust. Deadly sins. They could even get me killed. I got on my bike and rode on, but my mind was glued to the rocks, my "dog's" nose trained on the balls.

I passed the fire department. They must have an air pump, mustn't they? But could I be so brash, so brazen, so *shameless*, as to bother these guys with more important things on their mind than my trifling, touristy needs? I rode on. I found a gas pump near the public bus lot and tram cemetery where two dead trams were dumped. There was electricity for the electric cars but no air for me. I pushed on, reaching the lighthouse promontory. It was too hot and sunny today to sit on the wall. I breezed by the Octagon's 2'x4' pool and passed the Dayspring Church. No singing. My mind advanced to the community garden.

But in truth I was still obsessed with those balls. They sang to me like Sirens, the neon yellow fuzz pulsing in my brain. I could just see it. I'd be lost, drowned, or arrested attempting to retrieve them. What a stupid fucking way to die. I would win the latest "Darwin Award," a ball clutched in each rigor-mortised hand, a crazed dog look frozen on my face.

I checked the walls and fences out as I rode around. Some were lower, some were higher. Who cared? It was the wall and fence *by the balls* that mattered. I made my decision to return to the scene of my future crime, cased the wall, and found the courts.

There were staff around...what for, the tennis court...the island? Would *they* arrest me...yell at me? A police car was parked with lights flashing (it turned out to be someone unloading stuff out of their trunk with hazards on). No, no, it was *good* people were around. They could save me if I was trapped! I surveyed the scene. Where were the balls? I located one and my heart jumped. It was tantalizing, clean, bright, and new, just waiting to be saved from a watery death, to be spirited away, licked, and chewed like all good tennis balls deserve. But I could only see the one. Where was the other one? Had someone taken it? If so, why hadn't they taken both? The heist was not worth it for one. This was definitely a two-ball job. Puzzled, I walked a bit farther and found it, parallel to the first, observable on the jagged black rocks only from the perfect trajectory. Visions of my mini dachshund jumping up and down with not just one, but TWO new sugar plums danced in my head. Isn't that what all good parents do when they travel, come back with gifts?

And yet, the restless urge still bubbling inside me, why did I *really* want to do this? Was I crazy? Obsessed? Insane? Perhaps the island itself with all its many hospitals had driven me mad. Perhaps the deranged spirits of the Octagon had attached to my body and possessed my soul.

Risking death, arrest, stranding, or just plain feeling stupid, I looked around one last time, and, relying on my boldness and athleticism, finally climbed under the fence and over the wall. I landed like a cat on the rocks. I looked back quickly at the wall behind me to assess the height. Too late now. I'd have to climb it to live. I kept going, moving out on the large black rocks that edged toward the East River (an estuary, actually; the water flows in several directions). In fact, earlier I noticed a feisty tidal whirlpool up river I'd not seen during my last visit to the island. The water turned this way and that, like a wave pool. I was grateful not to be in a dinghy. It was a treacherous vortex; one of those "big water" events that could suck you in and drag you down. The water by me here was calm. My challenge was the wall, not the whirlpool.

I seized ball number one, then quickly snatched up the second. A flash of joy and the thrill of success raced through me. I took that adrenaline, put the balls in my pockets, and hoisted my foot on top of the wall. I grabbed part of the fence to pull me up. It was too low. I reached for a taller part. It was too high. I grabbed the lower one again and hurled my weight up, like a pole vaulter, both legs to the right, on top of the wall. I crouched then slid under the fence. The heist was complete. Was I being observed? Of course not. No one gave a shit.

Emboldened by my triumph, I went for more gold. I rode back to the fire station. It was deserted. I peered around the several trucks. Did they have an air pump? There was movement inside, a tall man. Feeling a bit like an idiot, I pushed my luck. "Is it too stupid or obnoxious to ask if you have air for my tires?"

The tall man stepped out of the dark house. He was older. Good-looking. He reached up and pulled down a small hose. "That's what this is here for." He filled my tires *for* me.

This was a full service station. I refrained from asking him to wipe my sunglass lenses. I asked his name and shook his hand. "Thank you, Steve. Stay safe. Stay cool." This was Wonderland all right. Everything I needed was right here.

Now, to The Flora. The community garden was directly across from the station house. I was filled with joy. Everything was working out easily and effortlessly. My boldness and bravado had been rewarded. I wasn't insane, I was *fantastic*, hurtling walls to retrieve plundered treasure for my tiny dog! No boring summer day, this. I had created a masterpiece of adventure and intrigue. I parked my bike in the shade, said a quick prayer for its protection, then entered the garden. The sun was blazing hot so I stayed only long enough to hear one crazy gardener yelling a rant at his speechless, seated compadres. A battle in a beautiful community garden? (Yes, it's still New York City). At least there were no corpses composting. I exited, jumped on my bike, and headed toward home.

The tram was fixing to lift off as I arrived. The doors closed. No biggie, the next would leave in eleven minutes. But the attendant saw me and stopped the packed tram. He opened the tram doors and the gate for my bike. I skootched in.

The same little girl with the same cute escort was on my return ride. Her skin was bright red now from the sun and the heat. Her earlier inquisitiveness had metamorphosed into crankiness. She gnawed on a plain bagel. "I want to go to my home now!" she cried. Then, eyeing a guy in a wheelchair, she started to blurt something blunt but her chaperone quickly reined her in. Speaking to her quietly, he quashed her very public pronouncement and handed her the purple sunglasses, but she was no longer interested in the dazzlers.

I liked this little girl. We weren't too different. Loud mouth, bold personality, and pale skin. She had purple shades and the cute guy. I had contraband and full tires. My plunder was bulging from the front of my shorts. This is a look you can't help but notice, not unlike, say, someone stuffing a ripe banana in their front pocket.

I retreated when we arrived on my island to give egress to the baby carriages, wheelchair, and the cute chaperone with the little girl. He and his cranky charge left the area last. He did not look at me, nor did she (still red, hot, clutching her bagel, and unaware I had enjoyed both of her USO Tram Performances). Like many a bewitching starlet, her glamorous entrance to the island was supplanted by her irascible exit. I, on the other hand, had succeeded in creating divine adventure to escape my hot house arrest. I made a triumphal entrance once home, having scored the prize and seized the day. I was my doggy's hero. And mine, as well.

CHAPTER 19

Falling Together

I'm Chicken Little. My uterus is falling. No, not literally. A friend of mine experienced that precise condition as a result of her propensity for continual breeding, and, after her third child, had to have her uterus tucked up in a bun with surgical bobby pins. Since she wanted to both a) keep her uterus inside her body cavity and b) have more kids she shifted over to fostering, then adopting two more babies. As she'd already amassed a large conglomerate of bunnies, chickens, cats, and dogs, her choice to yet again expand her human brood led me to observe to her eldest teenager when I learned of the second adoption, "Your mother is a hoarder." I'm not sure she got the joke.

So, back to my uterus. I have fibroids. Fibroid tumors. A relatively common affliction for the American female, they may affect between fifty to eighty percent of the population. They are benign, and can cause symptoms ranging from excessive menstrual bleeding to cramping to difficulty in conceiving, depending upon how big, how many, and where they are on the uterus. I have had fibroids at least ten years and they were medically monitored up until six years ago when I still had a corporate job and its associated health insurance. I have lived much of my life without health insurance. It's not affordable for me. So I trust in my karma, and thus far I've done fine getting occasional tune-ups from my chiropractor, medical intuitive, and acupuncturist (whom I fondly and collectively refer to as my "witch doctors"). I rely on good nutrition, homeopathy, vitamins, herbs, exercise, and common sense to keep me healthy.

However, not long ago, when both my chiropractor and medical intuitive palpated my lower abdomen then looked up at me, eyes bulging, and expressed deep concern regarding the large, hard mass, I took note. My chiropractor said meaningfully, "You should get this checked out." I knew what he meant—by an M.D. I knew, presumably, that they were fibroids. They were also, presumably, bigger than when they were last medically checked via sonogram, six years ago when I had insurance. But they wouldn't kill me. That is, if they were still what I thought they were. If things had progressed *only* in the direction I knew. What was going on inside, in that dark, mysterious cavern? I needed a spelunker. Did I also need surgery?

This was a terrifying prospect for me. I'd never had surgery. I contemplated my options and a doctor/ pre-existing condition/surgery wasn't one. I couldn't afford health insurance, plain and simple. It was health insurance or the rent, not both. I swallowed my fear and resolved to heal the condition with acupuncture and Chinese herbs.

My acupuncturist asked me what I was eating. "None of your business," I blurted. Not to be rude, but I eat really, really well. Whole grains. Organics. Greens. Vegetables. Fruits. Natural sugars. Yes, I drink coffee. Yes, I drink wine. Yes, I eat organic dairy, as well as antibiotic and hormone free meat (for the most part). I was not interested in being told I needed to become vegan, macrobiotic, or gasp, give up coffee, wine, or dark chocolate. I've become increasingly healthy over the years, having been given a great head start by my health savvy mom (a follower of Gaylord Hauser, Adele Davis, and *Prevention Magazine* from decades past) and slowly recovering from my own adolescent rebellion/going to college/trying to eat well in a society that hasn't for decades (hence our myriad health crises, both physical and psychological). Something is off. I'm not the only one who's sick.

While I balked at writing a food diary (a totally useless waste of time by my account, "Dear Diary, Today I had a piece of cheese and SEVENTEEN HUNDRED CRACKERS"), my acupuncturist managed to get out of me what I'd had for breakfast that morning. An organic egg, some whole-wheat toast with organic butter, and iced coffee with soymilk.

"Soy milk?" Her eyebrows immediately arched. "How much soy do you eat?"

"A lot," I replied proudly.

Being a tortured, conflicted "protein-aholic" who loved animals, someone who craved meat but felt terrible about eating it, I was always relieved to nosh on a protein source that was non-animal derived. I was a vegan "wanna be." In fact, I love vegan food. Some of it is five-star great. And let's be honest, *plenty* of non-vegan food is just plain terrible. Bad cooking is not limited to any one style of food. In New York City, Candle 79 (stupid-ass name), Angelica's Kitchen, and Caravan of Dreams are superb vegan venues.

I bought every damn soy product Trader Joe's stocked. Soymilk. Soy creamer. Soy infused tortilla chips. Soy infused cereal. Edamame. Soy cheese (disgusting, to be sure). Soy sour cream. Soy cream cheese. (Not as bad as soy hard cheese, but it certainly doesn't taste like cream cheese. It tastes like white.) Soy ice cream, soy cheese blintzes, soy veggie burgers, soy "chicken" nuggets, soy breakfast patties, soy sausage, soy bacon, soy sauce, soy protein bars, soy protein powder, good god, I could go on, because, in fact, *soy is omnipresent.*

It turns out that soy can produce excess estrogen in both men and women. And estrogen grows fibroids (in women only, as they grow on the uterus). Quite simply, I was growing a virtual fibroid forest in my abdomen; with soy "miracle gro" tossed on the soil every couple of hours, and routinely watered with soymilk. Not to mention that most soy is GMO in this country, so add the GMO tumor factor into the soy/estrogen/fibroid mix. If GMO does not mean something scary and terrible to you yet, do *five minutes* internet research and get on board with the rest of us Monsanto-hating activists. We're supposed to be eating *food* from Mother Earth, not *chemicals* and science projects from Big Pharma (which, it's been psychically predicted, is due soon for a big shakedown on the order of what our banks, insurance companies, and world economies are facing).

"Medicine" is supposed to make you better, not keep you sick. But drug companies like *customers*. Big Pharma is, to me, the biggest, baddest drug pusher around, pure and simple. Many cures are available that are *not* being released because products alleviating the symptoms of those dread (but curable) diseases are very, very lucrative. Do the math. Drug companies are not altruists any more than "homeland security" keeps us safe. (Did you know that "homeland security" was a little phrase Hitler's peeps came up with? Shouldn't that tell you something right there?) "Homeland security" keeps us in fear, and

Big Pharma keeps us addicted. They go hand in hand, do fear and dependence.

So while acupuncture did not cure my fibroid problem, my practitioner alerted me to the dangers of excess estrogen both from soy as well as meat and dairy products because (factory) farm animals are routinely injected with growth hormones, not to mention the antibiotics which are making us all resistant to treatment by medical antibiotic pills when we really need them. And seriously, people, get over the germ phobia. Stop using hand sanitizers and stop bleaching everything. Bleach is terrible for you, your kids, your pets, and our environment. It is a toxic chemical. Most household cleaning products are toxic, and they end up right back in our drinking supply. Just *wash your hands*, okay? A little soap. Good germs abound. They're *supposed* to. Killing them is killing life. Being unhygienic is another matter altogether. All that hand sanitizing shit is going into our water supply and wreaking havoc on our ecosystem. Please buy all natural household cleaning products (*not* "green" by Clorox, for God's sake. That's like buying vegan cookies from Exxon.) I use vinegar, orange oil, Bon Ami, and a few all-natural brands to clean house. And *please, buy only organic, humanely certified meat and dairy products*. For you and the dear animals who give their lives and bodies to us. I now step down off the soapbox, returning to my diminutive five-foot stature.

I had cultivated a fibroid forest so colossal that it had its own zip code and heartbeat. (I could feel a throbbing pulse in my lower abdomen, some vein or artery, and it was so distended that I looked pregnant and could not do exercises on my stomach at the gym.) Was some of the "pooch" fat? Yes. Was all of it? Not by a stretch. This was a baby I would never deliver. How the fuck was I gonna get rid of it? I had no idea what actually lurked within.

Add to that the fact that half my big toenail mysteriously fell off. (I didn't recall a brick falling on my foot, and if it had, my toe would have turned black and blue first, right?) When weeks later I noticed the white part at the top of the nail on one pinkie (pinkie, that's a silly little word, now isn't it?) expanding from the normally thin line to an extended semi-circle, plus a tiny patch of yellow at the base of the nail, the base itself now slightly depressed (physically, not psychologically), I flipped out. I realized it must be the dread nail fungus. For a gal who keeps her nails neatly trimmed, generally unpolished, and does not go to nail salons, how the hell did this happen? (You're probably thinking I should have used some hand sanitizer, huh?)

I knew a girl who had nail fungus. Her nails were an unsightly mess. She wore nail polish to cover up the fact that the nails on all ten fingers and toes looked like oyster shells or Italian sfogliatelle (a many layered pastry). She was convinced she caught it at the nail salon, but continued to go to one, and brought her own tools from then on. (New York City subsequently changed the law so that salons couldn't do any invasive scraping or cutting of cuticles or dead skin). She was obsessed with weight and image, generally, so this was a terrifying hardship for her. Her father was an M.D. She said they'd tried every drug to no avail. It didn't look too good for me, someone not particularly obsessed with looks *and* without a doctor.

I went to Whole Foods and asked if they had natural treatments for nails. The young man showed me nutritional supplements to strengthen the nails. I lowered my head in shame and inquired specifically about the dreaded (vocal volume dropped) "nail fungus." He kindly and brightly escorted me to the "nail fungus" section then added that some people just use tea tree oil since that's a main ingredient in some of the products. My heart soared. This was curable with my arsenal of "magic tricks!" I didn't have to buy a thing, perfect for my micro budget. I have tea tree oil at home. (Tea tree oil is an antifungal and a great cleaning product if you want to add a couple of drops to your homemade cleaning brew.) I jumped online again and looked up natural cures for nail fungus and found that apple cider vinegar, rosemary oil, eucalyptus oil, among other natural remedies were considered corrective. I took a bath in Epsom salts and added a few drops of eucalyptus oil to the water. I now have a mild case of hives on my back from the oil. (Essential oils are extremely potent and one must be very sparing and careful with their use. More careful than I was.) Best to put the essential oils directly on the digits themselves (or in a hand or foot soak) for this purpose. Sigh...

How in God's name did I get nail fungus? And why in God's name did it only affect my right big toe and my left pinkie? My best guess was the dark (and cheap) reflexology joint I went to in Chinatown to treat the cripplingly painful plantar fasciitis (an invisible inflammation in the feet) that had been plaguing me for the past six months. My Chinese reflexologist "Brian" could neither pronounce nor spell his "American name," as he wrote BRAIN on their business card. (My natural cures for plantar fasciitis? Ice, aspirin, stretching, chiropractic treatments, and time.)

Between the fibroids, fungus, hives, and plantar fasciitis, I was but a wave away from sinking like "The Wreck of the Edmund Fitzgerald."

Since years of vitamins, herbs, acupuncture, and castor oil packs (look them up online) had clearly not cured my fibroids, I became convinced that surgery was inevitable. At the suggestion of, and with the encouragement of friends (some of whom had been on, or were on it themselves, unbeknownst to me) I now contemplated the unthinkable—applying for Medicaid. I was utterly torn up about this option. Medicaid was something that simply had *no* relation to my life. It was for "other" people. Poor people. Dependent people. I'm an independent people.

I had a roommate a few years back, a talented photographer who worked like a dog to rustle up business. He contracted Lyme disease, which progressed to Bell's Palsy and froze his face. He went to Bellevue, a public hospital. He got a social worker. And he got Medicaid. What was he supposed to do? It was pay the rent or have health insurance. Some people really are doing the best they can to take care of themselves. I'm an independent person waiting for royalties to kick in from my first book, *Raving Violet*, (now out, as of the publication of this, my second book) as I continue to drain my life savings to survive. I'm not a menace to society. I've paid taxes for years. I've paid into social security *and* unemployment, and, in fact, my boss had to *command* me to apply for unemployment benefits when he laid me off (I thought unemployment benefits was for slackers, too).

But according to Mitt Romney, I represent All That Is Wrong With America Today. Yessirree. Not only am I the 99 percent, I am also part of his select, infamous *subgroup*: Mitt's 47 percent made up of slackers, moochers, users, grabbers, and takers. Mitt looks upon me like "Hester Prynne." Come on, Mitt, pin that S*carlet Letter* of shame on my chest! Better yet, I, along with working Americans (who struggle and wonder *daily* how they will get by let alone thrive the way multi-billionaires like you do, with off-shore accounts squirreled away around the world like little acorns) showed you up on Tuesday, November 6, 2012.

It's okay, really, if Mitt wants to call me names. I have a few names for him, too. Like, "Mormonic." And "Adolf Mittler," since he'd love to get rid of me and the rest of the scourge of society he finds so deplorable.

Now, speaking of Mormons I have to recommend this fabulous little documentary called *New York Doll* (2005). It's about "New York Dolls" bass player, Arthur "Killer" Kane, one of the first, essentially, punk rockers, who, when fame released him from her clutches, went on to become a Mormon librarian in Los Angeles. Of all things. You've never witnessed a stranger life trajectory, with additional plot twists and turns. It's touching, funny, and beautifully produced. Now back to Brother Mitt and our regular program.

Being born with money isn't the problem. *Having* money isn't the problem. *Having no compassion or regard for your fellow man* is the problem. Franklin Roosevelt was born to money, so was his humanitarian wife, Eleanor. Teddy Roosevelt had money but he still cared enough about the environment to preserve its beauty by starting our National Parks system. The Kennedys had plenty of money but Jack and Bobby were peaceniks and fought for civil rights, as Franklin and Eleanor had before them. The word humanitarian cannot even remotely be applied to Brothers Bush and Romney. Like "Agents" in *The Matrix*, they are "Exterminators." Yes, that means they view people like you and me (the non-Mormonic) as viruses to be killed. Send us off to war. Saddle us with debt. Turn us into wage slaves. Addict us to the drugs your companies make money off of. Keep us fat and sick with drug-addled, pesticide and toxin-filled genetically modified processed food. It's a perfect recipe for our failure. And Halliburton's success.

Medicaid is the "dirty little secret" for those of us who have it but don't wear it out on our sleeve like a badge of honor because it's *not*. It's stigmatized, no two ways about it. The need for basic medical care by those who can't afford it is a badge of *shame*. I couldn't even contemplate applying for it until I weighed the stigma against my own growing conviction that my growing growths needed surgical removal. Surgery won.

I received a New York City public school education. How is health care so different? Should you feel ashamed if you don't feel well or if you don't know something? Andrea, a dear friend of mine from high school, is a fellow New Yorker who now lives in England and works as an administrator for the NHS—National Health Service, the UK's socialized medicine program. She says it's fantastic and has been the happy recipient of their services. Michael Moore's swell documentary *Sicko* provides all the auxiliary evidence you need. *Escape Fire* is a new documentary about how our "health care system" is neither healthy, nor caring, nor an effective system. It suggests wonderful new models by qualified professionals.

Like any good mother, why *shouldn't* this country provide the best opportunities (the arts, education, healthy food, and healing for the sick) for her kids? Certainly the rich do this for *their* children. They give them every possible opportunity. It's not called spoon-feeding or infantilizing *then*, is it? Do I advocate socializing everything? No, I advocate *prioritizing* life-affirming causes, instead of the war, in-fighting, and fear mongering we've been intentionally addicted to. We spend trillions subsidizing worldwide murder via our evil (but lucrative, for Dick C$heney and Halliburton) Military Industrial Complex.

Would socializing positive change be the worst thing in the world? Look at Jimmy Carter's beautiful work with Habitat for Humanity. Real Americans care about *all* Americans. Real humans care about *all* humans. Most people *want* to take care of themselves, to be independent, given half a chance at a good, satisfying, and challenging life. (Factory and minimum wage jobs do not qualify for this). We do not offer that opportunity to most of our citizens by depriving them of, at a minimum, a good education. We have been encouraged to value guns, fear, isolation, uniforms, vigilance and "flash" over study, learning, community, creative expression, and happiness.

My parents and their parents survived the Depression in New York City. They lived in rent-controlled apartments. My dad finished up his college engineering degree at NYU via the G.I. bill. When he died, I received (rather paltry) social security payments as the minor of a deceased veteran. My mom took out a government loan to help pay for my college education. My family had received government assistance in one form or another over the decades.

Benjamin Franklin, Thomas Jefferson, John Adams, Alexander Hamilton, George Washington, and our other Founding Fathers and Mothers (yes, *Mothers*. Who do you think kept the home fires burning? *No* war is suffered or fought by men alone.) did not risk life, liberty, and their considerable personal fortunes to create *this* country so that Americans could work for minimum wage to barely afford the crap food that induces diabetes, obesity, heart disease, and early death, all so we could waddle over to Walmart on a Friday night. That is not the American Dream but it *is* the American Reality for many, many of our brothers and sisters. My father did not volunteer to fight the Nazis and fly extra combat missions to protect That America. Ah yes, my soap box again. I descend. Again. Clomp, clomp (high heels).

My sister had fibroids surgically removed to facilitate her getting pregnant. It worked, but it was no small deal, this surgery. We're talking IVs (I've never had one), catheters (same), and being in a hospital for days. Who would take care of my dog and cat and who would take care of me? I sustained a high level of fear and anxiety worrying about it all. I cried in the gym when I could no longer comfortably do something as simple as a sit-up. My uncertain fate loomed.

My mom had fibroids, too. They did surgery to remove them and found she had pancreatic cancer (which subsequently killed her). My mom and sister at least managed to squeeze out two kids. Not me. Not yet. This was a loaded topic.

Mom's dad died of Hodgkin's disease, the same cancer that killed Jackie O. Mom's mom had stomach cancer. Mom said, "They opened her and sewed her right back up. There was nothing they could do." Cancer was a family tradition.

I was at a séance four and a half years ago, desperate to know about my love life (still idle four and a half years later, my desperation has dissipated into a coma). I was hot to trot, having just met someone I felt there was potential with. I was itching for info. I needed my peeps on the other side to cough up the goods, especially since my mother had come through at another séance right before I'd met this guy and had said that a relationship would start the next month and it did. I met him. I liked him and knew in my bones I would see him again. But I haven't. Yet.

So I was ready to throttle the dead for info. If I could have wrapped my hands around their little ectoplasmic necks, I would have. The medium pointed to me in the darkened room and said, "Your grandmother who died of cancer is here." Mom's mom. Thank God. A message! "She says you are not going to die the way she did."

What? Who cares? I'm not afraid of dying! I'm afraid of DYING SINGLE!

Preparing mentally *now*, years later, for surgery, I took comfort in that message. To the best of my knowledge, all I had were huge, gangly, ungainly, benign tumors. For me to enjoy the rest of my natural, single life.

Since not knowing is worse than knowing, I imagined the worst. A midwife pal of mine palpated me in a public toilet. (Yes, I'm always good for an anecdote.) We were at a restaurant. We went into a private, handicapped bathroom. She had me sit on the toilet, perpendicular to the normal position. She asked me to lean back against the wall. The handicap bar was in the way, and the toilet was near the wall, so I did my best acrobatic act, hanging from under the bar, leaning back as far as I could so she could palpate my abdomen. The verdict was in. She said, "Well, you have at least one the size of a baseball." And that's just one. When I had them checked 6-7 years ago there were some inside, some outside, and even one "pedunculated" (one of the strangest words I've ever heard, but how can you forget it?). I think of it like Florida, just sorta "hanging off" the edge of the States. "In medicine and zoology, a peduncle is an elongated stalk of tissue." Stalk? I was the botanical or zoological specimen, hanging from the handicap rail in a public toilet like a vine or a primate brachiating amongst the branches.

My midwife friend urged me to get Medicaid and get it checked out. I applied.

As my readers know, I am keen on metaphysics. When I discussed the possibility of surgery with my dear friend Diane, she called back and told me that if I needed it (and yes, I was petrified of the prospect on every level, from the logistic to the surgical) that her husband would drive her into the city (she hates the city) from New Jersey and that she would take care of me. That is a true friend.

She is also hooked on metaphysics, and while she had given me psychic messages before, she'd never given me an outright-channeled one. That changed with this:

"This one, Valerie, carries great energy within her. This energy, when channeled through the heart will create much that is beneficial. However, she has created an unwanted growth in the body in the area of creativity and birth. In the process of soothing and comforting herself while living through a trying earlier time in her life, this one has created a false growth. It has been nurtured with very strong and consistent thoughts and feelings regarding the creation of an experience that is not in her lifetime blueprint. When the growth is taken care of (we see a medical procedure) a new outlook will prevail and she is most capable of starting anew. This one has been steeped in the clearing and cleansing of accumulated experiences and learning what self-love is made up of in an earthly life. We see this one spreading her wings and leaving the cocoon in which she now lives. She will be stimulated in taking a greater step in her life journey which will offer her much of what is needed in a more enriching environment. This one, Valerie, is greatly loved. She will surprise and delight herself when the opening for energy flow is created and a life well lived in ease and joy is made manifest. Go in peace."

I always acknowledge the inner workings of Spirit, karma, and my own mental belief patterns that contribute to my health issues. The second, "sacral" chakra (where the tumors are) is the color orange, and symbolizes both sexuality and creativity. Of course they are connected. The very act of creating life comes from sexuality. While acknowledging my karmic issues, the simple fact remained that a medical procedure was indicated, and I was convinced this meant surgery.

Even once on Medicaid, it took me 8-10 weeks to get an appointment with both a general practitioner and an ob-gyn. After six years of no medical attention, frankly, I wanted the fibroids removed yesterday. As scared as I was of the surgery itself, I face my battles head on. However, late September and mid-October were the earliest dates I could nab. My neighbor Shirley, a senior, reminded me it's the same with "real" doctors, too.

My GP appointment was at 7:30 p.m. on a Monday night. I've never had a medical exam at night, have you? I chose a smaller clinic rather than one of the larger public hospitals because I hoped I might get more personalized attention. From the minute I arrived at the clinic in Union Square I felt blessed. Blessed by God, blessed by Spirit, blessed by the State, blessed by Medicaid. I was utterly grateful. I was grateful to the people running the clinic, good and kind people all. I was cognizant of the other patients around me, whatever their private missions. We all had our reasons for being there on a Monday night.

I loved the guard. I loved the staff. I tried to love the patients but they seemed unhappy and preoccupied, other people with Medicaid, or perhaps no insurance at all, going to a clinic rather than a "regular" doctor or hospital. Here we were, all in it together. When the front desk clerk asked one patient what she was here for the girl froze and muffled something under her breath about not wanting to say out loud what it was. Her pants were already dropped low enough. No need to take them off altogether.

It was night. There was filtered water to drink. The place was clean. And quiet.

I arrived early and filled in my paperwork. I was then ushered into the back area where I would be seen by the doctor. I didn't have to wait long before a nurse with a thick Jamaican accent came to take my temperature, weigh, measure, and interrogate me. I didn't want to look at the scale (I don't weigh myself) but when I peeked I discovered that I weighed the same as my dad (a diminutive fellow) during WWII, a number I'd just reviewed that morning, as "chance" would have it. Sobering. Who wants to have *that* in common with your dad? The nurse then measured me at *under* five feet. I'm too young to shrink.

I demand a recount.

She asked an inscrutable question. I asked her to repeat it. "Do you take the *tobaccah*?"

"Oh! Do I *smoke*? No, I don't…take the tobaccah."

"Do you take the alcohol?"

"Yes. Yes, I do take the alcohol. I'm a wino. Or a 'wineaholic' as I prefer to call it."

"Drugs?"

"No."

"Do you feel hopeless or helpless or like ya can't go on?"

"Well, sometimes, but not in a 'kill myself' sort of way. Thanks for asking." I was rather enjoying this adventure at 8 p.m. on a Monday night in Union Square, NYC. Someone was finally taking care of me.

My doctor introduced herself. She was being trailed by a female medical student. They were both very nice. I joked that, given the hour, I'd contemplated bringing a bottle of wine and some cheese. I told her I needed surgery. I described my symptoms and she decided that not only did I not need surgery, but that no treatment was indicated at all as the fibroids would naturally go away on their own, especially with the onset of menopause, which she felt would start for me in ten to twelve minutes.

When I explained to her that the fibroids really do cause me distress and discomfort, if not out and out pain, and that I could easily be many years away from menopause, she then suggested that I try the Mirena IUD, which contains time-released progesterone. She said it was the first line of defense against fibroids these days. (I must add here that I subsequently discovered that the Mirena does not *shrink* the fibroids, as I had hoped it would, it only helps to diminish the excessive bleeding, a *symptom* of the fibroids.) I was still in a state of shock that she didn't think I needed surgery. She hadn't even examined me before she gave her prognosis. Would a sonogram be ordered? No. Though I could live without the invasive trans-vaginal sonogram where they stick a "wand" up your twat while your bladder bursts with the quart of water they insist you drink beforehand so "everything" shows up clearly on the monitor.

I asked if she would at least touch the mass before I left. She did me one better. She said she'd give me a full gynecological exam. I was baffled since she was my GP, but this is a family clinic—there isn't much they don't do there. She felt my abdomen and had the medical assistant do the same. She commented that my uterus was very large.

When she prepared to do the internal exam they had to go on a field hunt to find a lamp. I didn't even see stirrups on the table. I visualized hoisting my legs up without them. (Thank god I do sit-ups.) When they finally stumbled back into the room with the lamp, knocking into the examination table, (the curtain obscured exactly where it/I was) the light wouldn't work. Lying on the table, I offered to push the plug into the socket to see if the connection would stick, and joked that next time I was bringing my own lamp. I was just grateful someone was finally examining me. So it was like a scene from *MASH*.

Doc asked the nurse to bring her some "scoopettes."

The nurse stopped, "What's a scoopette?"

The doctor looked at me and rolled her eyes. "It's the long Q-tip type thingie?" The nurse left the room. Doc says, "She's been here two years already. You'd think she'd have a clue."

"How long have you been here?" I inquired.

"Eighteen years."

Doc then embarked on a field trip looking for my cervix. Given the abnormal growths, the entrance to my uterus had migrated. Somewhere. My cervix was askew, like a mouth puckered to one side of the face. She found it eventually. For all I knew, my uterus looked like Quasimodo or a creature from *Alien*. She took notes in case I wanted to schedule the Mirena IUD procedure, and she would be charged yet again with attempting to locate my roving cervix.

"The *procedure*?" I blurted. "That's what you call it?"

"Yes, inserting the Mirena is a procedure."

I was ecstatic, convinced that this was what Spirit had predicted *and* prescribed for me. Not surgery, but a medical procedure that would provide me with a steady dose of progesterone to counterbalance my overabundant estrogen. Based on my fears, I had jumped to conclusions regarding what Spirit meant.

Not wanting to "milk" the system, I declined their kind offer of tetanus and flu shots (more to the point, I don't believe in vaccines). Doc then pulled out the model of the Mirena and its inserter for a little "show and tell." It looked like a tiny fishing rod, but the line was all tangled up because the thing was broken. The IUD itself is a little Y made up of what looks like a red plastic coffee stirrer. She tried to reel the line in to show me how it works.

"You fly fish?" I quipped. My ass was gonna be saved by a Y-shaped coffee stirrer inserted with a fishing rod.

I left the clinic two hours later on cloud nine, high as a kite on "scoopettes."

I called a few friends to fill them in on the good news as I walked home on the balmy night. I strolled by lovely Gramercy Park, my feet barely touching the ground. My friends were relieved, knowing how worried I'd been about the mystery in my midriff. My midwife friend had not heard that the Mirena was used to treat fibroids, and she was concerned that a sonogram had not been ordered. She suggested I try to see an ob-gyn friend of hers instead of the ob-gyn appointment with a nurse practitioner I'd scheduled for mid-October at another clinic. If her friend took my "insurance," then she would be able to discuss my results with him.

I was reticent. First of all, he's a guy. I haven't had a guy gynecologist since I realized…I didn't need one. When it comes to that kind of personal maintenance, it's a girl thing. I don't want anyone down there unless we're dating. Second, despite my fears concerning who/what/how I would be taken care of via Medicaid, I was doing pretty well so far. I trusted my karma, my fate, and the MBO prayers I regularly say. (I.e., "I request a Most Benevolent Outcome, that the perfect doctor give me the perfect treatment for my fibroid healing, whether surgical or not, and may the results be better than I could hope or expect." Thank you, Tom T. Moore, MBO mentor extraordinaire.) Lastly, it took me ten frickin' weeks to get *this* appointment. Did I really need to wait another ten weeks?

The problem was solved when I discovered her doctor friend did not take my "insurance." On top of that, he'd not heard of the Mirena IUD being used to treat fibroids, either. Was it possible, just possible, that I was getting cutting edge treatment at a clinic, on Medicaid? That, in fact, this doctor with 18 years (she looked to be in her 50s or 60s) in the trenches, in her very own Mobile Army Surgical Hospital unit, might know some shit that the fancy doctors didn't? This cutting edge technology was saving me from literally being *cut*.

When I got home, my intuition prompted me to immediately look up *natural progesterone,* as my procedure was not scheduled for three more weeks. If progesterone was the cure, I wanted to hit the ground running. I ordered some inexpensive natural progesterone cream (with ingredients like lavender and avocado oil). For extra measure I ordered high dose vitamin C, because I believe it can help everything without hurting anything. Within a day of applying the cream I was cramping and got another period on the heels of my last one. (Things have not been normal in that department for some time, due to the fibroids.) My stomach has already shrunk. I am losing weight. Look up the health advantages of natural progesterone cream and see if it might benefit you. Along with B6 and folic acid, I am (yet again) taking my health into my own hands. I am confident that I am on the right track with this progesterone thing. I feel like a million bucks. My fears had transformed into a fascinating odyssey.

The very next day after my clinic appointment I ran into a girl I'd not seen in a good six months. We used to regularly bump into each other walking our respective dogs. Since she's a girl of approximately my age (give or take 5 or 10 years) she's old enough to be afflicted with something like fibroids. I figured I'd fill her in on the potential miracle of natural progesterone cream and the

Mirena IUD and save her from the horrors of surgery someday.

Too late. She, who was well funded and had the best insurance and medical care money could buy, described to me the horrors of her experience. First of all, her fibroids caused her to drop *buckets* of blood at the drop of a hat. This was inconvenient, not to mention messy. Perpetual hemorrhaging is hardly an alluring pastime. Though petite, very attractive, and "well-maintained," she looked to weigh 80 pounds, and apparently survives on iced coffee, cupcakes, and yoga.

Her doctors recommended a D&C, which did not help. When they decided to operate, her doctor ordered the dreaded "trans-vaginal" sonogram to locate the biggest fibroid so that he could make the incision on the appropriate side of the uterus. His staff could not locate the fibroid. They had cameras up her canal, and a team of technicians could not map it accurately. The doctor stormed in and did it himself.

The surgery was major. It's essentially a caesarian, sans the baby. Unlike the usual single baby, multiple fibroids can grow inside, outside and within the walls of the uterus. Tricky stuff. Especially if you want to preserve the uterus so you have the option of getting pregnant. Many women get this surgery in order to facilitate conception.

They wanted my friend to stay three nights in her private hospital following the surgery. She was fortunate to have parents who took care of her dog. She was also fortunate to be able to spring for a private room, at an added cost of $500 a night out of pocket. When she waddled (catheters and IVs and surgery, ohmy) in excruciating pain over to her private bath, she discovered that there was dried blood in the toilet and on the wall. Not hers.

The bathroom in my clinic was pretty clean.

It was no accident I bumped into this girl the very morning after my salvation the night before. Her story represented the very worst-case scenario I'd been petrified of. She'd been traumatized. Her experience was a nightmare from beginning to end. So my escapade the prior night had incorporated a bit of *Keystone Cops* and *Marx Brothers* routines. I viewed the chaos fondly, appreciating the fact that these women (as the clinic was run predominantly by them) and their patients, are doing the best they can with what they have. Like any good soldier or MASH unit does.

On a bright note, the essential oils and apple cider vinegar seem to have stopped the nail fungus in its murky tracks. Score one Australia (tea tree oil's motherland). Please explore natural cures such as chiropractic, acupuncture, castor oil packs, healthy nutrition (including eating yams for natural progesterone), vitamins, and herbs. They have much to recommend them. Most of our drugs are *based* on natural cures (watch the new documentary *Sacred Science*). Hippocrates said, "Let thy food be thy medicine and thy medicine be thy food." Do research. Trust your intuition and do the inner work, too, the soul-searching, dream interpretation, "What does this malady symbolize" stuff. Explore your situation from different angles, including seeing a doctor when you need to.

I never thought I would be sharing a story about my innards, let alone the even more intimate story about the insurance. (Sex isn't the final frontier of privacy. Money is, right, Mitt?) But, ultimately, if somewhat chagrined, I'm also proud. I took care of myself. With help from my friends, and yes, the government. I am grateful. There's nothing like feeling sick, alone, and scared, with nowhere to go. Do you want your friends, neighbors, and fellow citizens feeling that way? I sure as hell don't. And as the marvelous Elizabeth Warren rightly asserted in her Massachusetts Senatorial campaign, no one, *not one person ever* made it *solely* on his own. We all ride on the coattails, and very often the shoulders, of others.

As I deal with my own recession and health challenges I reaffirm my dignity as a human being, an American, not passive and "entitled," but one whose rights to life, liberty, and the pursuit of happiness remain intact. Entropy and chaos reign before systems are rebuilt. I am, in fact, falling together.

CHAPTER 20

Chasing Rainbows In A Hurricane

I live alone. Have for years. I sleep alone. Write alone. Eat alone. Read alone. I drink alone. Think alone. Listen to music, meditate, bathe, ponder, pontificate, vacuum, scry, and nap. Alone.

That being said, I'm a rather profoundly happy person. I've worked long years to get that way, and the prospect of surviving a hurricane, or imminent surgery (that's another story) by myself, has long been a way of life I'm comfortable with.

New York City is nice and quiet right now. We're in the midst of Hurricane Sandy. We should be good at this now, having weathered Hurricane Irene just a year ago. I bought water then. Candles. Filled my bathtubs with water in case we had a power and water outage. (Imagine, not having water during a hurricane?) Hurricane Irene gifted my neighborhood with a gentle mist in which I took a lovely walk. After the "fray," I downed gallons of purchased water in post-precipitation penance.

This year, I bought no water. I purchased cream cheese. Not because I needed it. But because it was organic. And on sale. A friend called me from coastal Florida, prime hurricane land, but she's on the gulf and Sandy free.

"Are you prepared?" she inquired.

"I bought four tubs of cream cheese. The answer, is yes."

She asked me if I had an ice chest I could store food in, in case the power went out. I used to have one. It was cute. I *bought* it because it was cute and I hoped to go on picnics. I never went on a frickin' picnic so I finally donated it to the Salvation Army. Who knew I'd want it for a hurricane some day?

Since I was ice chest free I decided to turn the temperature down in my fridge to the lowest setting to make sure everything was extra cool for longer in the event of a power outage. When I happily approached my Florida grapefruit this morning they were frozen solid. I put the bag out on the floor and gave them all CPR. I turned my fridge temp back to normal. Hurricane be damned.

The city is quiet. No raging storm and no traffic. The city shut down mass transit last night at 7 p.m., well before there was a drop of rain. We had a little pitter pat this morning then a little more in the afternoon. Yeah, there's some wind. But we've had flash floods that have done worse damage in ten minutes than I'm seeing outside in 24 hours. So, some yellow leaves have been ripped prematurely from their trees. Boo, hoo.

I got a call from Texas checking in on me, an email from London. I am alone, yet not. I have friends. I am loved. I am enjoying the peace and quiet this storm has provided thus far. The peace and quiet that I provide me.

Via Facebook I learned to my surprise that Red Hook Brooklyn is under water, as are parts of Connecticut and New Jersey. I'm on the tenth floor of a high rise in a non-evacuated zone. So far, so good.

As I sat down to eat my early dinner tonight, something, I don't remember what, inspired me to get up and look out the window. Perhaps the wind was blowing harder, perhaps I heard a sound, but the event eludes me at present. Out of the corner of my eye I caught a colorful parachute swirling and descending. Was it a rainbow colored paraglider? It was circular—a big balloon? An enormous, pliable pool float? What was I beholding in the deepening dark?

It was a large, rainbow colored circle, but cylindrical, not a sphere. As it blew in the air I discerned that it was a blow-up baby pool, hurled off a terrace from my building or some other high-rise nearby. Or maybe from miles away. It is a hurricane, after all. I got the sense that this blow-up pool had been newly liberated from its home, not having guardians sufficiently intelligent or caring or nearby enough to batten down the hatches and put a brick on the darn thing. It flew by my window the way Dorothy's house flew out of Kansas. I hope the baby's okay.

Now, I am excited by plunder. I find things often and make good use of them. Be it a quarter, a MetroCard, or a bag of cash. (Yes, I found one, but not as big as the one the friend of a friend found, which still remains my dream. Large, new, unmarked bills.) I'm rather ingenious with a find. I had wanted a splash pool for my mini dachshund, and while I don't yet have the terrace or yard that should rightly accompany such a possession, that wouldn't stop me from grabbing if the right splash pool should blow by my window.

I watched the rainbow colored circle blow in the wind like a kite, stories above the street. My first instinct was to dash down and retrieve it when I saw it land square in the middle of First Avenue. But then a car ran over it. Splat. What good is a smashed splash pool? But then the circular rainbow made lift-off again and landed again in the middle of the road. Should I run down and retrieve it? Oh, heck, my dinner would get cold, right? But this was intriguing, and my sense of adventure was piqued. This was a hurricane! And this was my hurricane escapade! Who cared if my dinner got colder, half of it was cold to start with. On the other hand, how much did I care about a smushed rainbow-colored blow-up plastic pool for my dog? I sat down and ate.

Still curious, I got up to look out the window again. The circle blew west and exited my eye line. I sat down to eat, again. Dinner completed, my sense of adventure unabated, I jumped up with adrenaline. The wind was howling now, and it was really raining (almost like a hurricane) not the piffly wind and mist we had earlier. That was it. I grabbed my raincoat, threw on my trusty all weather clogs, and ran out the door. I was chasing the rainbow.

Now, a good ten, fifteen minutes had gone by since I first saw the pool. (I'd not had a three course meal with music. Actually, I had, it was simply consumed at a brisk, hurricane-like pace.) The rainbow-colored blow-up pool had been calling to me like a Siren from the minute it blew startlingly into my vision. I had to have her. Or at least try.

No one was particularly rushing out of my building at this point in the storm. Nor were they rushing in. No one was around. Not even on the street. There were very few cars. Where could she have gone? Since I last saw her blow west, I looked to the west, toward the sidewalk in front of the school. Nope. I looked on the avenue. It had been fairly obvious there when I saw her lying immobile from ten stories above. Nothing. My intuition drew my feet downtown. I was getting wet, even with my raincoat and hood on. Big deal. That's what storms are for.

The Chinese restaurant was still open, still with the ridiculously high price for lobster posted in the window. (Who eats that?) Everything else was closed. The supermarket, the banks (obviously). I didn't see anything open, really, just a few shops closing. It was 6 p.m. Time to close on a stormy Monday night. I walked south two blocks, peering left and right into the streets, looking for my rainbow. Nothing. I looked down steps and up platforms, and toward the large blue pool housing a fountain in front of the big apartment complex. Wouldn't it be funny if the blow-up pool floated in the big fountain? Sandy did not agree with my sense of humor. The kiddie pool was not there.

I was tiring of my adventure. I was plenty wet and the wind was picking up. I didn't need the pool, I'd just needed to try. I needed to get out of the house and into the fray. I needed an adventure. I felt truly detached from my desire to find the rainbow, the rainbow in the storm. I just loved the idea. The search was enough. Made me smile.

I looked left-right once more as I approached my building. I walked under the scaffolding ten yards from my entrance. I was ready to be home, satisfied from my adventure. There she was. Lodged under the bumper, between the two front wheels of a parked car. There was my runaway flying rainbow splash pool.

I pulled the rainbow out from under the axle. It was blackened. Not from the storm, the street or the underside of the car but from the mildew/schmutz that had been allowed to grow not only inside but outside the basin. This rainbow had been abandoned long before the hurricane. It didn't take but half a second for me to make the decision that it was neither cute nor pretty enough to warrant scrubbing the thing inside and out, all to offer my dog an (other) dog toy in an apartment now filled with such things.

I met a medium once who looked into my eyes and said, "I see an apartment scattered with pet toys." This was a medium with powerful vision. Listen, if I could get my dachshund a slide, I would. But that'll have to wait for the house in the country. A pool and slide are best suited to a yard, not a living room.

Between wanting to give it a good once over before relinquishing it a second time and being the concerned citizen that I am, I hoisted the yucky toy out and pushed it securely in the trash can with a lid on the corner. It would not (likely) blow away again. It had reached its final resting place.

I returned to my aerie to snuggle with solitude, tinker with thoughts, wade in words, consort with cream cheese, and reanimate dead grapefruit, while visions of swirling rainbows and hurricanes yet danced in my head.

CHAPTER 21

Hysteria, Redux

Hysteria: Agitation, Delirium, Excitement (from Greek "hysterikos," of the womb, suffering in the womb)

Redux: Restored, brought back (from Latin "reducere," to lead back)

My uterus's life is at stake. It is in detention, on probation, and very possibly, on death row. I've requested a stay of execution. Despite my attempts at humor and bravery (in previous chapter "Falling Together") it seems I really am falling apart. I was trying to be philosophical about my health issues in past missives and put a positive spin on everything. I am, in fact, both falling together and apart. Change is like that. Not particularly neat, or clean. The old must die that the new can be born. Birth, now there's a topic.

This saga is ten, maybe twelve years old when benign fibroid tumors were first detected in my uterus. Back then when I had corporate-job-covered health insurance, these growths were monitored via sonogram. There was nothing to worry about. At the time.

When I had something to worry about (the growths had grown) I sought help. Now that I have coverage, I am getting everything checked out. Twice. My general practitioner offered to give me an internal exam when I told her about the fibroids. She observed, via palpating, that my uterus was large and high, and she invited her intern to feel it, too. She did a pap smear. I didn't tell her that I had a regular ob-gyn appointment scheduled in three weeks, and that they'd be doing that very test again. After six years of no medical attention, if the guy on the corner offered to give me a free pap, I would have taken it.

The only test I declined was the mammogram. Controversy alert! I'm about to express an opinion you may get up in arms about. Since x-rays are dangerous, it's my belief (and others too, complete with evidence) that they can cause harm, even cancer. Don't get your knickers in a twist, ladies and gents. If you want one, get one. I'm not discouraging you. I'm just expressing my inflammatory opinion. I had a few mammos in my time and have decided I don't want any more. I just don't like 'em. And it's not that I'm a pussy, but rather that the idea of crushing and radiating sensitive breast tissue just doesn't, well, seem *healthy* to me. There's no way in hell you'd get men to submit their *balls* to a similar procedure. I trust my fate/karma, and the cysts that have been detected (via palpating) in past exams have always turned out (via mammogram) to be nothing. So I'm sticking with that. Remember, you have a say in your medical regimen, and what tests and treatments you submit to.

Six years ago when my doctor begged that I get a mammogram, I held my ground. I finally agreed to a breast *sonogram*. My breasts get cystic around my period. It's normal, not cancer. This recent wave of gynos produced one referral for a mammogram that shall remain but a nice try on their part. I've got bigger fish to fry. No tit squishing for me, thank you very much.

So it was my chiropractor (Dr. William Zev Roizer, NYC, I just love him to death) who first clued me in to how bad the fibroids had gotten. He palpated my stomach. "Your stomach shouldn't be that hard," he said earnestly.

"You mean, that's not my six-pack" I gulped, "underneath my fat?"

This took me back to my twenties, when I was in a play with an "older" married woman. Linda was 32 and funny as hell. A former alcoholic, she joked about her drunken Connecticut relatives with the most ridiculously waspy names I'd ever heard (and could never remember). We played sisters in an Off-Off-Broadway play. Linda and I both loved cats and shared a smartass sensibility. We'd both suffered enough in our young lives to understand things that others couldn't. She always made me laugh.

"Feel this," Linda said to me backstage. She took my hand and put it under her right breast, just under the ribs. It was hard as a rock. "Does that seem right?"

I touched myself in the same place. Squish. "Uh, no, that doesn't seem right."

Linda had cancer. I don't remember what kind. It was March.

When Linda was dying she had a last request for me. To take her record of Vince Guaraldi's *A Charlie Brown Christmas* and put it on cassette for her, which I was happy to do. I made a copy for myself, too.

Linda died just before the next Christmas. She spent the last few weeks or months of her life with a relative in Hawaii. I spoke with her once while she was there. The next time I called, she was gone.

So, hard things in soft spots. Not a good thing. I wasn't worried about dying. What I worried about was losing my uterus. You see, everything has come late for me in life. Love (still waiting), parenthood (still waiting), professional success (on the cusp). My spiritual beliefs are very strong, culled from a variety of sources, including channeled readings, psychic readings, mediumistic readings, and my own dreams and intuition, which are very strong. My faith is unshakeable. I believe it is in the cards for me. However, as my age "tips the scales," not many people believe what I do: that it is possible I will give birth. Naturally. No bells and whistles.

Now, try explaining this to a doctor. The first one wanted to do nothing for my fibroids since she believed (based on what?) that I was about to enter menopause (thank you very much, but I beg to differ) and that the fibroids would then diminish on their own. My period is now irregular, and I am what Chinese healers call, "a reckless bleeder" (sort of like a reckless driver but with more blood, less alcohol). Some of this could be perimenopause, based on my age. But some of it, for sure, is the effect of the fibroids. They can make you bleed like a stuck pig. Fun, if you're into that sort of thing.

The first thing this doctor did was run a blood test to make sure I'm not anemic. I'm not anemic. The second thing she did was suggest the progesterone filled Mirena IUD. I asked if it shrunk fibroids and she said, "It's the first line of defense against fibroids."

What else could that mean but that progesterone would help shrink them? My midwife pal and her ob-gyn friend had never heard of it used that way. But I was excited about it, believing it would help, and obviate the need for (dreaded) surgery. I felt it compulsory to tell each (incredulous) doctor that I believe I might have kids some day and that whatever treatment they prescribe must take that into account. I not only want a uterus at the end of the day, I want a viable one. This was Joan of Arc time. No doubt about it. They all looked at me like I was nuts, except the nurse practitioner who said to me, "If you are still menstruating, and still ovulating (I am), then you can still have a baby."

At least I could say to the doctors, "Look, I know you're going to think this is crazy, I'm well aware of the statistics, and my age. But this is what I believe. I want to leave open that possibility. So you have to know about that, crazy as it may seem to you, before you prescribe treatment."

Convinced that the Mirena IUD was going to shrink my fibroids, I scheduled the procedure. Couldn't wait to get going. The procedure was to take no more than 45 minutes from beginning to end, that's how long my appointment was scheduled for. I figured between checking in, paperwork, a urine test (to make sure I wasn't pregnant) the insertion of the device itself should take 15 minutes. It was like putting in a tampon, right?

My good mood took a slight downturn when I asked the intern how long it would take for the IUD to shrink the fibroids. She didn't know. It took another downturn when a young male intern was invited in for my final consultation before the procedure. I was relieved he was not invited to the "insertion party." I'm not a fan of male ob-gyns, though he was a very nice young man. I gave him my card and told him to read all about my uterus on my blog. He left, I'm sure, very confused by me.

There were three women present during the procedure, and a fourth (was this a quorum?) gave me four Advil to take, two of which I partook of, and saved the other two for later. This was going to hurt? Advil Girl didn't answer me and walked out. Doc and the intern went "down south" and the third young lady was there to support me and hold my hand while they were doing the mechanical stuff. This was when my mood took a *big* downturn. When they opened me up I was in immediate pain. They cranked that speculum open wide enough to allow a Mack truck through. My body immediately convulsed with excruciating pain. Though lying down, I was weak in the knees, quivering in pain from head to toe. I stared helplessly through teary eyes at the young lady holding my hand to my right. This was like labor and delivery. Except there was no baby.

Because my fibroids are legion and large, they have contorted the alignment of my cervix, which is no longer facing south as it should, it is now southwest. The doctor could not complete the insertion, I'm not sure she could even start it, but she was no quitter. She asked for a contraption to dilate my cervix since obviously my "other" opening was cranked to capacity. The pain remained at unabated, excruciating levels. When the doctor finally admitted to me that the IUD wouldn't even shrink the fibroids, it would just lessen the bleeding (thanks, but that won't help fix my uterus) this became beyond a lost cause. She pulled out a hypodermic to shoot my innards with painkillers. Thank god I couldn't see what they were doing. Experiencing the effects was brutal enough.

The doc said "Oh, I just want to get it in, I hate to quit!"

We were going nowhere fast except deeper into a bloody pit of pain and despair. I said, "It's enough. Please stop."

When they left the room it looked like the scene of a crime. There were bloody sheets, mats, pads, metal tools, and a huge hypodermic needle lying about. I had been there two hours. I walked out onto the cold sunny streets of bustling Union Square and sobbed. It was like an abortion gone bad. I was still no farther along in getting my tumors treated. Since the Mirena's primary purpose is birth control, I finally concluded Doc prescribed the IUD just to make sure this loopy broad *wouldn't* get pregnant.

Life went on. I got long overdue physical therapy for a knee injury years ago resulting from a brutal bike accident I'd had just as I'd lost both job and health insurance. The leg had been x-rayed. There were no breaks. But the knee is brimming with ingredients other than bone. These things were crackling, crunching, bending, and hurting. I awaited the knee specialist's opinion. Without an MRI, he manipulated my knee and put me through my paces. He proclaimed my knee structurally sound, and prescribed four weeks of physical therapy to strengthen the muscles and correct the pain I'd been having. He prescribed frozen vegetables on the knee after I did my exercises at home. I was already icing my foot for plantar fasciitis (yes, the "falling apart" theme). Now I had okra on my knee as well. But I was getting better.

I went back to my old school, Hunter College Elementary, to speak to sixth graders about being an actress and writer. I was mortified when they invited me. In fact, when they sent out the announcement that they were looking for architects and historians to talk about New York City, I felt safe responding, "Sorry I can't help! Just an actress and a writer."

They responded, "See you Friday."

Since I am a public speaker, and I wanted to get my philosophical clutches on those little kids, I said, "Okay."

I was assigned a student ambassador and tour guide. Isaiah was groovy and deep beyond his years. He wanted to be an actor, which is why he had requested the gig with me. Isaiah has already been in a Sunny-D commercial, so he's already a pro, and earning more than I am as an actor. He was utterly charming and prepossessed without being ingratiating. He had a puffy golden afro that framed his face like the corona of the sun. This kid had an *aura*. I assumed he was in the sixth grade like the rest of the kids I'd be speaking to after the coffee welcome and my school tour. Turned out he was in fourth grade. This kid was the sun itself. Bright, warm, confident, and relaxed. He grabbed a danish and poured himself a cup of coffee. Cream and sugar. A couple of his fourth grade compadres joined him and started a coffee klatch, probably talking about the Russian Revolution. These kids were bright, poised, and well mannered. Best of all, they still acted and dressed like kids, not divas, moguls, hockey pros, and hookers. There were only a few of us returning student grownups there. A teacher finally breezed by and froze, aghast, "Are you kids drinking coffee? You're not supposed to be drinking coffee!" She wasn't really mad, and they weren't really bad. I found it rather charming, like the toddlers of France drinking wine.

Isaiah took me to the basement and showed me the hangout room where ISAIAH was sprayed big in purple graffiti, but almost at the ceiling. He didn't say anything but I did. "That you?" He nodded his head. "How'd you get up there?"

"My dad did it. He's an actor and a graffiti artist."

"Cool."

When I stopped to run into the bathroom he said, "I gotta pee, too." (I said it first.) We sprinted left and right into our respective facilities. He yelled after me, "Don't forget to wash your hands!"

"Okay, Isaiah. I won't." I couldn't stop smiling.

We popped our head into the first grade music class. The teacher immediately invited us in; she'd met me at the coffee klatch upstairs. She was playing the piano for a group of little cutie patooties who were singing a song with the assistance of a lyrics chart and two charming and animated young ladies. The song was about diversity. They sang verse after vivacious verse, including, "Some have one daddy. Some have two." Could you die? I was so proud of my school. I made a little speech to the first graders then Isaiah egged me on. "We still have a lot to see before your talk in 14 minutes."

Maybe this kid could be my manager someday. Nah, he'll have his own empire. Fourth grade!

I encouraged the sixth graders to follow their bliss and be wary of staying at jobs they hate. Since both writing and acting are fields rampant with rejection, I told them to figure out ways to make themselves feel good and emotionally sound throughout their lives. "Go where the horses run, and where the doors open. Follow opportunity." These sixth graders, whom I was expecting to be socially precocious, looked like second graders. Isaiah had a bigger persona than they did (hey, he's the actor). I ended up fielding career questions on behalf of their parents. "Is it better to quit a job you hate before you look for a new job, or to look for a new job while you're still at a job you hate?"

Isaiah told me a teacher had been picking on him because she was racially prejudiced. He said his dad went up to her and said, "Leave my kid alone."

She felt threatened and said she was going to call the principal.

Isaiah's mom added, "Call the cops!"

I thought that was a cool thing Isaiah's dad did. Dad had his back. When I was a student at the school there were lots of racial issues and the teachers did nothing about them, not wanting to make waves. When we toured the high school I saw more kids, and I do mean kids, they looked like children to me, of every race, creed, and color. We were pretty integrated when I was there, but now there were Asians, Muslims, you name it. It was a virtual

UN in the middle of New York City. Truly, New York City is the UN of the world.

I went back to the hospital for two sonograms, one internal, one external, to determine the size of my fibroids. My female Russian tech made no comment about what she saw while we chatted pleasantly, her sono-wand probing my insides. She was gentle and kind. When I didn't hear back from my nurse practitioner (she told me to call four days after the test to get results) I crashed her office on my way to physical therapy for my knee. There she was. I assured her I wasn't stalking. But I was really rather desperate to get the show on the road. It had been 12 years. If I needed surgery, I wanted it as soon as possible.

She took me into her office. The fibroids were huge. My request for surgery was reasonable. She helped me set up an appointment on the spot, for Halloween. I was relieved. Then Hurricane Sandy hit. My consultation with the surgeon was cancelled. My hospital had shut down, as had many in downtown Manhattan. I prayed to get rescheduled as soon as possible. My prayer was answered.

I was met by a Russian doctor. He kept insisting he was Georgian, but I associate Georgia with peaches, pecans, and drawls, not men whose first name is Grigol. He seemed a little serious, but I also caught him smiling. He told me he was going to examine me internally again and do a biopsy. After my last trauma at the clinic and the IUD, I shuddered at the thought. I also thought this would be a consultation, not another show and tell. I asked if he would give me painkillers. He said I wouldn't need any. I was not so sure.

Well, like it or not, here I was with a male ob-gyn. He said the sonogram showed polyps inside my uterus, and they had to test them.

"For cancer?" I asked.

He nodded. Nobody likes saying those words, but I don't pussyfoot around. We all know what we're talking about, don't we? Spit it out! This guy was gentle as a lamb with a speculum, much more gentle, in fact, than the last female ob-gyn I'd seen (although my nurse practitioner was perfect in that regard). He had to stick a thin straw into my cervix to get a sample. He was very apologetic about hurting me. He didn't hurt me at all. When he wanted to get another sample he called for the dreaded "dilator." Oh god, not that. Well, in came reinforcement, his mentor (my guy was a fourth year resident) an Indian doctor. A very jovial fellow. I sat up, shook his hand, and thanked him for looking at my face *first*, since everything else was exposed for the world to see. I welcomed him to my "uterus party." We were off to a rousing start.

Russia said he'd called for a dilator but India was like "pshaw, gimme that straw." He shoved it up quickly and expertly. Yes, I felt some discomfort. But he got what he wanted. Phew. It was over. But no. He grabbed another straw and shoved it up even harder this time. More discomfort, maybe even a little pain. But this, too, was over quickly. "I wanted to get a good sample!"

Okay, doc! They palpated my stomach and India said I was 20 weeks pregnant. With tumors. He left the room.

I told Russia my tale about "maybe babies." "I know this sounds crazy, however…"

He asked me questions about my health and habits. "Do you drink?"

"Yes, I drink a lot of wine."

"This, I do not count."

My kinda guy. My pal David said, "He probably doesn't count vodka, either."

Russia consulted with India and came back with the consensus. "You have zero percent chance of getting pregnant." I kept my mouth shut and listened. "You are going to get anemic from all this bleeding. If you don't do a hysterectomy, you are at risk for endometrial cancer and we will have to test you for that every six months. If we remove your fibroids, you will grow new ones and come back in two years wanting more surgery." Was he quite finished?

I told him I still wanted my uterus, baby or not. He went out and returned with reinforcement, his mentor. I faced the firing squad. I said, "First, I am aging very slowly." They acknowledged my point. "Second, I am very healthy. I eat well and am in great shape." They listened. "I'm not worried about cancer. I'm also on an anti-fibroid diet now, whereas two years ago I was eating stuff that contributes to growing them." Then I pointed at India and joked. "You want my uterus, don't you!"

He pointed and joked back, "Your uterus has my name on it!" They warned me that even if they attempted to do what I wanted, which was to remove the fibroids only and leave the uterus intact, that if I bled uncontrollably (it's a bloody organ) that they would have to do a hysterectomy. I told them I understood. I may be crazy, but I'm not unreasonable.

They tried to scare me further by saying we have to wait on the polyp test results (I haven't heard from them, so they must be negative) and that my insurance might not want to pay for such a frivolous (implied) procedure. Silly me wanting to remove myriad tumors yet keep my uterus!

I was very upset when I left the hospital. I felt like a throwaway. They didn't perceive me as a viable mother, or even a woman. They asked if I was sexually active. I retorted, "No, but fingers crossed!" All very embarrassing. I was fighting for a cause only I believed in, with no reinforcements.

All the odds were stacked against me. Clock ticking. Still single, not a man in sight, and I'm advocating for the well-being of my uterus so I can maybe get pregnant at an age when most women don't expect to expect anymore. Well, I expect differently.

I exited the hospital during the city's first snowstorm of the season. I sat in the park and cried. There was nothing to say to anyone, no one I wanted to talk to. I just needed to sit. To be without a uterus, which would mean the immediate onset of menopause, was just not something I was prepared for. I went to the hospital to get fixed, but not like a dog.

I asked Spirit for inspiration in my dreams. I got it. I dreamt of a tiny baby elephant (actually, a bunch of 'em) baked in porcelain dessert dishes in my oven. They were so precious, so darling, even in death. It was a sad sight. I looked at one as I pulled it out of the oven. It sighed. I wasn't sure I saw what I saw. It looked up at me, slowly. It was alive. I couldn't believe it! Against all odds (my goose was cooked, it was a bun in my oven) this baby beat all the odds. I knew then that my wish had a chance. Then, of course, I wondered where the hell I was gonna put an elephant.

I received the "inspiration" the next day to advance my case with the doctors by responding to a few more of their arguments to which I had not responded in person. They had left me hanging in mid-air. Would I even get surgery? Would insurance agree to my request? When I called to leave the doctors voicemails, the front desk said that neither doctor had voicemail. I found this hard to believe but I was not interested in alienating her, or anyone there for that matter. "How can I best communicate my messages to them?"

She asked me what I wanted to say. She listened then took it upon herself to book my appointments then and there. "Of course insurance will approve this! And if you want your uterus, you keep your uterus!" Girl Power.

My neighbor Shirley said, "Do the doctors know about the surgery?"

I replied, "The doctors will find out when Denise tells them!"

She booked my pre-surgical testing (2.5 hours) and my pre-surgical consultation with one or both doctors. She booked my surgery. And she booked my follow-up visit two weeks after surgery. She was God's answer to my cry for help. My "inspiration" to leave them messages was what led to Denise getting the ball rolling, exactly as I wished. The day for surgery she offered was the very first day when all my commitments in November and December were over. There was Kismet written all over this "baby." Add to that my dream *that* night that a Russian mobster was coming to torture and kill me. I was petrified. I asked him what he was going to do.

"Torture and kill you!" he said.

Yahoo.

Within a few minutes this man had not only become my friend, but my ally and protector in the dream. Out went my worries about my Russian surgeon. I am confident that he will truly be on my side and advocate for my wishes.

When I meet with the boys in a week I have a few things to say to them, things I did not get to say in person or in voicemail. "I do not have zero percent chance of getting pregnant. However, if you take my uterus, I *will* have zero percent chance of getting pregnant. You haven't tested me for fertility, and I didn't ask you to get me pregnant. In fact, I was ovulating the day you examined me. Whether or not I have a baby is between me and God. Whether or not I have a uterus is between me and you."

The Georgian is Russian Orthodox. I'm counting on his faith to leave room for mine.

I want my uterus. Whether or not I have a baby, I believe in the holistic wisdom of the body. Menopause is not a disease. When my body is ready to enter it, naturally, perhaps after a baby or two, perhaps not, I will welcome that passage. That is the time of a woman's "Wise Blood" when she heats up and starts transforming alchemically, according to the indigenous peoples (read *Woman At The Edge Of Two Worlds* by mystic Lynn Andrews). My uterus got a little derailed. Frankly, I got a little derailed. But I'm back on track. I want my uterus to graduate with the rest of its class.

Another meaning derived from hystera/uterus/womb is hysterical. As in "very funny." As in uncontrollable fits of laughter. After all the hoops I've jumped through, mystical (I'll write about those another time), medical, and surgical, I hope to be laughing my ass off after all is said and done, after my uterus is "reducare" (restored), brought back to health and viability. Maybe I'll even bring a bottle of vodka to the operating room.

About the Author

Valerie Gilbert is an actress, solo performance artist, and story teller now translating her ability to make others, laugh, cry, and sit on the edge of their seat into a writing career. Born into an ardent metaphysical family, she is passionate about exploring the depths and heights of the Divine Mystical Human Experience. She shares this enthusiasm with others via her books and blog, "Raving Violet," and the weekly meditation and psychic development group she leads.

An avid environmental, animal and peace activist, Gilbert is a native New Yorker, Harvard graduate, and member of the Dramatist's Guild. She lives in New York City and is now a popular audio-book narrator on Audible.

www.ingramcontent.com/pod-product-compliance
Lightning Source LLC
Chambersburg PA
CBHW052018070526
44584CB00016B/1805